Indiana Statewide Association of Rural Electric Cooperatives, its member electric cooperatives, and *Electric Consumer*, the publication of Indiana's electric cooperative community, are pleased to present *The Quiet Path: Covered Bridges of Indiana*.

Through photography, poetry and prose, electric cooperative member Marsha Williamson Mohr and her father, Maurice Williamson, explore the beauty and history of these endangered structures scattered throughout rural Indiana.

Since the member electric cooperatives of Indiana Statewide provide electricity and other value-added services to rural and suburban communities all over the state—including most of the communities fortunate enough to lay claim to the covered bridges—we are particularly proud to play a role in producing this unique volume.

For over 50 years, *Electric Consumer* has shared stories of electric cooperative members, rural Indiana treasures, energy and utility issues, and information about the benefits of owning your own power company. And for almost 70 years, Indiana Statewide has provided a plethora of services—including government relations; training and safety education; management, director, and office skills training; public relations; and communications—to the local electric co-ops that serve approximately one-half million households and businesses. Those electric co-ops, some in existence since 1936, literally brought the lights to the country when other utilities refused to string electric lines to less populated rural areas. These REMCS and RECs continue to provide reliable service with unique customer service and community-minded perspectives.

Our longevity may not yet rival that of the covered bridges, but we're proud of our heritage of service, and of the lives we've impacted along the way.

Copyright © 2002 by Marsha Williamson Mohr

All rights reserved, including the right to reproduce this work in any form whatsoever without permission in writing from the publisher, except for brief passages in connection with a review. For information, write:

The Donning Company Publishers
184 Business Park Drive, Suite 206
Virginia Beach, VA 23462

Steve Mull, General Manager
Ed Williams, Project Director
Dawn V. Kofroth, Assistant General Manager
Sally Clarke Davis, Editor
Bridget Belmont, Graphic Designer
Scott Rule, Director of Marketing

Library of Congress Cataloging-in-Publication Data

ISBN: 1-57864-188-8

AVAILABLE UPON REQUEST

Printed in the United States of America

The Quiet Path:
Covered Bridges of Indiana

By Marsha Williamson Mohr and
Maurice L. Williamson

Table of Contents

Foreword..... 6
Preface..... 10
Acknowledgments..... 12
An Introduction to Timber Bridges.....14
The Essential Parts of a Good Bridge.....18

Adams County..... 20
Bartholomew County..... 22
Brown County..... 24
Carroll County..... 28
Dearborn County..... 38
Decatur County..... 40
DeKalb County..... 42
Fayette County..... 44
Fountain County..... 46
Franklin County..... 48
Gibson County..... 54
Grant County..... 56
Greene County..... 58
Hamilton County..... 60
Howard County..... 62
Jackson County..... 64
Jennings County..... 68
Lake County..... 70
Lawrence County..... 72
Marion County..... 74
Montgomery County..... 76
Owen County..... 82
Parke County..... 86
Spencer and Perry Counties..... 128
Putnam County..... 130
Ripley County..... 136
Rush County..... 140
Scott County..... 146
Vermillion County..... 148
Vigo County..... 152
Wabash County..... 154

Index..... 156
About the Authors.....159

Foreword

As a child, at an unusual age of eleven, I had this inapplicable knowledge of American geography. My dad taught me how to appreciate nature. Maybe this was why. My favorite television show was Wagon Train. I was fascinated with the mountains and southwest deserts.

Our family of four set out for a month-long vacation out west. Cots were converted into bunk beds by welding them together and placed in the back of our 1960 International pickup truck with a custom homemade topper on back. One box for clothes, one for food. Four abreast, we headed for the adventure of my lifetime.

I was the trip navigator. With a brownie camera I shot black and whites. Rocky Mountain, Mesa Verde, Grand Canyon, Yosemite, Redwood, Yellowstone, Bryce, Zion, Teton National Parks, including the Pacific Ocean, to name a few. Some scenes of which I will never see again in my existence. Being ambitious, intentionally dropping the camera down a cliff so dad would buy me a different one (I wish I could convince mom and dad I didn't kick it, I stepped out to run to retrieve it!) Eight thousand miles later and a box full of photos, I entered these images in the county 4-H Fair later that summer. Got a blue ribbon. Would have gone to state, but they didn't like the photos of my family looking into the camera.

I remember the autumns we went to the Covered Bridge Festival. Seemed to be a quiet kid at that time as dad was always conversing with someone he knew. Raindrops fell on my head as I admired the Mansfield Mill's rushing waterfall and turning power wheel. I stood glaring out the window of the covered bridge at this scene. A beautiful sight. My roots were formed.

As years pass, I invested in a good camera. Was too poor in my early adult years. Photography became my passion. Add my love for my rural roots and American geography, I was set.

Parke County became a part of me. I can't explain my obsession to this region, but it appears to be why I can't leave the state of Indiana. That county with fields surrounded by hills, farmers working their plots, open meadows between lush woods, one-lane gravel roads meandering around the county like a spider web. Off in the distance a hint of a covered bridge could be seen. I have to see the mountains at least once a year. I have to see Parke County at least once every season. The passion was engraved.

Now my husband Larry and I travel all over the country and Canada. Yes, I love the mountains. Yes, I love the ocean. But what overcomes me when I am out shooting? That barn perfectly situated in a valley with mountains surrounding it. That coal mine with it's weathered, pitiful textures what do I do? Shoot the mountain through the window. Add a few flowers and I have the exposure of my heart.

In 1999 I aspired to photograph all the covered bridges in Indiana. My own personal challenge. My own reward anticipating the bridge as I travel many of our rural back roads of my home state.

And not an easy challenge. Countless times I got lost. Too many broken moments not finding the bridge, only to learn it was dismantled and stored in a garage. Two trips to Vermillion County, I finally gave up the search for the South Hill Bridge. Not on a golf course. Not standing on the lonely supports I found miles from anywhere on a rural brick road (what an amazing road!) A man was fishing on the replacement bridge. I asked him, "What happened to the covered bridge that once stood here?" He reassured me I was in the right place, and he too, felt saddened by the loss.

When leaving in the mornings, I always checked the forecast, and tried for good skies. Not always optional. Also had challenges with the lighting. Not knowing the direction of the bridge or how it was positioned, I had to surrender to nature. Not perfect. Not enough time to make it perfect. Had to do the best I could under the time constraint offered me. So many miles to go. Fortunately, I already had photographed most of the bridges from Parke County. A few missed ones.

Wish I could have photographed each bridge in its prime season, usually being autumn. "Wonder what the trees around this bridge would look like in the fall?" I asked myself countless times. Seeing photographs from other photographers of certain bridges that were obviously more colorful than mine was frustrating. Couldn't be as each bridge at each perfectly sun filled, peak colored autumn day. Not enough time to make it perfect.

In some photos it might appear something is lacking. For good reason. Many a time I had to eliminate part of the bridge, or position a tree in front of it because of graffiti, or some obstacle that obviously would alter the quality of the image. For example, the Guilford Bridge. The photo only contains a small portion of the bridge. Why you ask? Because I didn't want to include the parking lot below it. Didn't have the luxury to wait for the sun to go on the other side of the bridge. Not enough time to make it perfect.

I ruined shirts and pants from sticker bushes and sprained ankles, as I trekked to the banks of the bridges, carrying a heavy tripod and several cameras; I was determined to find the best angle physically possible. Dodging traffic as people proceeded on their busy work days, countless miles traveling through busy little cities, or jamming city interstates, I loved every minute of it.

Mom and I, twice, two years in a row, attempted to find the Sanatorium Bridge in Parke County. It must be gone. After buying a new detailed back road atlas of Indiana, I noticed this bridge to be listed again. New publication. Must still be there. The second year we were determined.

We WILL find it. We HAVE to find it. Driving again, the road appeared similar; I looked off in the distance. "Mom, I think I see it!" I said. Amish were working in their fields. A little anxious, mom questioned me if I knew what I was doing, as I exited the gravel road to this undisturbed path. Glad to have four-wheel drive. A sense of euphoria came across both of us as we shifted back and forth in our SUV on the rough trail. We could see it. There it was. We were a bit haughty when we were photographing it. Wondered how many people had seen THIS bridge? Not many, we agreed.

Our next item on the objectives was to go to the Billie Creek Village Historical Museum. Three bridges there. Being a person not particularly liking crowds, had never been there. Nice place. Had to take a tractor/hay-type ride to get to the Leatherwood Bridge. Waiting for people to gather, I asked two of the local men organizing the ride if they knew of the Sanatorium Bridge. Lived there all their lives, and no, hadn't seen it. Didn't know of it. "We do," I boasted.

Such a difficult process, eliminating the number of photos for this book. Wanted to include many more, but there too, was a constraint. Asking dad for help, we differed in opinions and compromised. I like what I strive for, the masterpiece of the bridge arranged as an artist would arrange it. Dad liked the bridge filling the frame. Said you could see more of what it looked like. Tried to include a variety of different angles of the structures. Some front entrance, some from creek side. Some vertical, most horizontal.

My father, being the historian he is, knowing Indiana like no one else, traveling miles and miles during his near forty years at Purdue University, he was the obvious choice to write this text. I loved spending time with him on this project. My father who taught me to love nature. My father who motivated me to reach this impossible dream. A dream of a lifetime, a book on our beloved covered bridges.

Journey and accept the rustic stages
Drive to unknown venture
View, view for the chance to aspire
A structure of yesteryear

Imagine, if you can
The structure
Will it be ruby, white or other
Will it have a valley or barn
Or pasture nearby
Will it be weathered, faded or prime

What will I think about this bridge
A favorite?
A one of a kind?

As a child opening a gift on Christmas morning
I search for that same pleasure
Of a scene I have not yet visited
A scene of vivid significance
A memory of times far gone

—Marsha Williamson Mohr

Preface

For fear that some readers may take this book too seriously, I must tell you that this work is one of love for the beauty of America and its natural and manmade setting rather than any kind of technical dissertation immersed in some sort of lifeless categorization of covered bridges by type of construction, year, size, or geographic location. Surely, we understand and appreciate the superb engineering skills of those early builders, and do enjoy reading the literature of trusses, beams, and materials used and all the rest. This book, however, will dwell on the builder as an artist, not an engineer. Surely, we will identify the bridges where possible by their structural type, but will talk a lot more about the builder expressing his inner soul in what he builds.

As a matter of fact, we want to investigate in depth the ability of those men to faithfully transpose their own thoughts and attitudes into lastingly beautiful structures that enhance the countryside as well as provide structural utility. Some of the bridges are strong and purposeful in their stance. Others appear to have risen from the land, rough hewn and somber, without adornment, quietly melding with the nature around them. Some are almost Victorian in style, replete with bric-a-brac, cornice, and frills. If you are lucky, you will happen onto a covered bridge, bright and colorful, striking in style, like the first woodland wild flower of spring.

Pure and simple, covered bridges were a working part of the countryside. Some of them, I'm sure, were technologically much better than others. Some stood for centuries, enduring the torture of heavy loads, suffering through cataclysmic floods, fires, vandalism, and neglect. Other structures merely collapsed into stream beds, or gave up the ghost at the onslaught of the first big flood, just died a lonely death because of poor design, bad materials, or lack of maintenance. In later times, however, the mortal enemies of covered bridges have not been structural deficiencies, but pure neglect (particularly lack of funds during the depression years), and the need for their replacement by more modern roads and bridges to carry heavier loads. Those factors can be understood, but the insidious temptations to burn them, rip them apart, or steal their parts is not easily understood. Covered bridges are vulnerable creatures. They need all the love we can give them.

It is estimated that around ten thousand covered bridges were built in the United States in the nineteenth and early twentieth centuries. Between 400 and 500 bridges were constructed in Indiana. In 1930, 202 remained. By 1998, ninety-two were left. There is a real sense of urgency here.

There seems to be, or is it just my imagination, a quiet correlation between covered bridge style and the geography, topography, and traditional attitudes of the region. For example, New England with its sturdy Puritan stock, forested rugged landscape, and tidy farms and villages dotting the countryside, built beautiful and quaint covered bridges to emphasize the pastoral beauty of strikingly scenic land.

Move south to the bustling mid-Atlantic states to a land of busy cities and wide rivers such as the Connecticut, Hudson, Schuylkill, and Delaware, and you will find covered bridges of another sort. They needed bridges strongly built to span large rivers, and trestles that would carry heavy loads. They needed railroad structures as well as bridges for horse-drawn traffic. Most of the states leased their roads and bridges to private businesses so tolls were levied for passage. They were not pretty, they were colossal. They reflected the technology of their time and location. Sadly, most all of them are gone, replaced by superhighways and urban development.

The covered bridges of Middle America sit amidst fertile fields and country villages and they assume the look of the breadbasket of America. They are square, sturdy, conservative, and take on the red and white color of the great barns that share their space. More than any other region, they amalgamate the nature that surrounds them. They are icons of a peaceful world—as they should be.

Western covered bridges remind me of the cowboy movies that I loved as a kid. They are rough cut, unpainted, and rugged. You could run a herd of Herefords, horses, and cowhands by them and they would look right in place.

My point is this. Covered bridges have precious little utility in a fast paced modern world. They are the nectar that acts as a catalyst to make the skies bluer, the grass greener, and the place more beautiful in which to live.

Obviously, structural beauty was not the real reason for a covered bridge to be built. They were built to bind roads and pathways, a continuum of efficient travel. They leaped over fathomless chasms, quiet streams, and wide rivers with one singular purpose—to get to the other side.

My daughter, Marsha Williamson Mohr, has a rare talent to capture on film the beauty and purpose of the world around her. All the photographs in this book are hers. She has traveled Indiana for years to make this collection and has a picture of every covered bridge in Indiana that still exists. They are a tribute to her work, and to the wonderful people of this state for lovingly caring for these beautiful bridges. I thank them all, and especially Marsha for this work of love.

As you can well imagine, writing the script and the captions was the opportunity of a lifetime for me.

—Maurice L. Williamson

Acknowledgments

Back in our exuberant youth and precious little in the way of financial resources, June and I and the kids, David and Marsha, piled into the old Studebaker and later on, in an old pickup truck and a homemade camper with its burdensome load of tent, camping equipment of every sort, boxes of canned food, clothes in banana boxes, and headed out each year on the remote highways of our beautiful country, just to feel the thrill of seeing what was over the next hill, or walking in the footsteps of some historic warrior. Teeming cities, crowded interstates, and tourist traps were not on our agenda. We wanted to see America, just as it is. And we did, the exhilaration of discovering the beauty and the heritage left an indelible impression on all of us. We shall never forget any of it, ever.

David learned to love the land and he became a farmer, and a very good one at that. Marsha, with the cheap camera that we bought her, was amazed with the fact that she could record, for all to see, beautiful images of the things that she had seen. And she learned to do it very well, and has become quite well known for her photographs, regularly printed in national magazines. These things make mom and dad very happy and pleased.

This book on Indiana's covered bridges has long been Marsha's dream. She drives Indiana, from north to south, and east to west, to get photographs of every bridge, in every season, in the state. When she asked me to write the text, I grabbed at the opportunity. During my forty years working at Purdue University, I wrote hundreds of treatises, promotional pieces, and magazine articles, but never a book. It has been a challenge, and I loved every moment of it! But first, I had to school myself on the covered bridge business. I read all the books and articles that I could find. I studied maps, and I reviewed all her pictures in great detail. I bothered friends who know local histories of bridges. I melded all this into my thorough knowledge of the land, features, and people of Indiana. And, out came this book; we hope you like it.

Marsh Davis and Suzanne Stannis of the Indiana Historic Landmarks Foundation kindly assisted me to locate great references.

My friends Don Foltz of Clinton, George Waltz of Parke County, Eleanor Arnold of Rushville, and Keith Ruble of the Vigo County Parks patiently suffered through long phone calls.

Booklets and articles by the Indiana Historical Bureau, J. G. Jones in Covered Bridge Topics, and the American Society of Civil Engineers all were rich sources of technical data.

Several wonderful books provided great bedtime reading and were a wealth of background information. I appreciate the good work of the authors, and thank them for adding to my knowledge of the subject. They are:

American Wooden Bridges, Historical Publication Number Four, American Society of Civil Engineers, 1976.

Covered Bridges of the Middle West, Richard Sanders Allen, Bonanza Books, 1970.

Historic American Covered Bridges, Brian J. McKee, American Society of Civil Engineers Press, 1997.

Bridges of the Past, Historic Landmarks of Parke County, Bob McElwee, Flying Colors Printing, 1993.

Covered Bridges in Indiana, Wayne M. Weber FAIA, Northwood Institute, 1977.

I must, one more time, thank my daughter, Marsha Williamson Mohr, for making this beautiful book possible. It is a blessing that she shares her rare talent with all of us. Her photographs are indeed a precious heritage.

And, to June Williamson, my wife, I thank her for her patient work on the computer, correcting all my careless errors, and preparing the script for the printers. Bless her heart.

Larry Mohr, Marsha's husband, was a constant inspiration to her, and dutifully kept the home fires burning while she was out discovering all these bridges. In moments of doubt, he was always there.

And to all of you, thanks for reading the book. We hope you enjoy it.

—Maurice L. Williamson

I would like to acknowledge first of all, my father for taking the time and endeavor in writing this book, and teaching me how to fully appreciate nature. My beloved husband for putting up with me spending long hours at the computer or away from home shooting, not worrying when I am on the road, and for his countless hours at home working so hard doing the things I should be doing. My mother, for coming with me on trips and being a great companion, for taking the effort to learn the computer and typing the manuscript for us. Last but not least, I would like to thank my uncle, Quentin, dad's brother, for being one of my biggest fans and encouraging dad and I to do a book together.

—Marsha Williamson Mohr

An Introduction to Timber Bridges

For the sake of definition, a "timber bridge" in this discussion, is one that is built of rough, sawn, or hewn members without the benefit of any kind of protective covers. They may be set on wooden pilings, or on stone piers. It is thought that timber bridges were built very early in colonial history (the seventeenth century). We can assume the first ones were small and spanned streams to connect rude roads near the settlements. They may have been rough logs set on stones without any thought to longevity.

Soon, there was a need to bridge over much larger rivers and more complex trussing was needed to incorporate longer free spans in the structure. There are spectacular examples of these bridges over the Delaware, Connecticut, Schuykill, and other wide rivers. Ingenious bridge builders developed their own truss types with names like Burr Arch, Town Lattice, and others. There were arguments aplenty concerning the superiority of one over the other. As a matter of fact, all had their place in differing situations. Sparks from the steam locomotives were deadly enemies of tinder dry wooden bridges and many of them burned. Most of these timber bridges were built in the very early 1800s.

Shortly thereafter, the need to protect the trusses and timbers from the vagaries of rain and rot was apparent. At first, they merely covered the trusses and timbers with planks. Then, roofs were used to protect the floor as well as the supporting timbers. Finally, plank siding and enclosed portals were put in place, and the protection of wooden bridges from the elements was complete.

The traditional covered bridge was generally a product of the nineteenth century. The first, the Permanent Bridge, in Philadelphia, was built in 1805. Within the next century, nearly ten thousand covered bridges were built as the western settlement of America took place.

The geographic distribution of bridges was, oddly, in a very irregular pattern. Vermont had more bridges per square mile than any other state. Pennsylvania and Ohio were absolutely awash with this amazing new technology, with Indiana close behind. The West was obviously much later in the covered bridge business with Oregon clearly the leader in numbers built. It may be just poor record keeping, but is seems strange that a small state like Indiana had over five hundred covered bridges and little virgin pine timber, while Wisconsin had the north woods and few recorded wooden covered bridges. Many states had no bridges at all or at least no evidence of them.

The construction of covered bridges declined sharply in the later decades of the nineteenth century. The development of iron (steel) bridges sounded the death knell of the wooden bridge. They were easily built, carried much heavier loads, and were more economical to maintain. As covered bridges aged, they were replaced by the new iron structures. There were few proponents of the preservation of the historic old bridges. Few county commissioners saw them as a thing of beauty. They rotted away, were victims of fire, flood, and accidents. They usually were single lane and could not carry the heavy loads required by burgeoning commerce. They stood squarely in the way of progress in an entrepreneurial society. They had to go! (Oddly, the iron bridges are now suffering the same tragic fate.) Of the ten thousand or so covered bridges built, only a few hundred remain.

Just in time, individuals and organizations realized that there is more in this world than speed and technology. Covered bridges have become, in the minds of folks who understand the value of the beauty and history in our pastoral settings, icons of our heritage. They are the focal point of massive preservation efforts. Happily, we can now predict that most of the remaining covered bridges have been granted a new life in the American scene. Three cheers for that!

Indiana's Covered Bridges

The archetypical covered bridges of Indiana are representative of the artistic, historical, and romantic notion of what they should be. Of over five hundred bridges that were built in Indiana, about ninety-two remain. They are carefully rebuilt, strengthened, moved, painted, bypassed, and publicized. They are the centerpieces of fairs and festivals, picnics and reunions, and even memorials of one kind or another.

Indiana truly is a composite of America. Historic highways cross it, one being the National Road and the other the Lincoln Highway. The land is scenic yet unpretentious. Meandering streams, winding country roads, colorful hills and valleys, and thriving farms give Indiana an obvious "country flavor." Neat little towns, country churches, and pretty farms, all make Indiana one of our really beautiful states. There, you have it. What a logical place for covered bridges.

The first major Federal highway in Indiana was the Old National Road, winding its way from Hagerstown, Maryland, to St. Louis, Missouri. It crossed central Indiana from Richmond on the east to Terre Haute on the west. It crossed a plethora of north-south streams and rivers, and many bridges, most all of them covered bridges, were needed. The first covered bridge built in Indiana was on the National Road, in Henry County, in 1834. In 1835, the second Indiana bridge was a large one built over the Whitewater River in Richmond.

The flood (not a good word to be used in reference to bridges) of construction of covered bridges began in Indiana. Some accounts relate that around five hundred bridges were built in the next twenty-five years, and the pace increased until about 1880 when the wooden structures began to be replaced by iron bridges. The last covered bridge built in the state was the Edna Collins Bridge in Putnam County in 1922.

It is impossible to accurately document the number and location of Indiana's bridges. However, we know that the geographic distribution of bridges was not evenly spread, by any means. The greatest activity seems to be in a belt across the central and south central part of the state. If a record of known and existing bridges is any measure, Parke, Putnam, Rush, Franklin, and Shelby Counties were far ahead of the pack. Topography may have been one of the reasons. The presence of streams that ran counter to most of the major roads was another reasonable explanation. However, one might suggest that the bridges were more common where most successful builders lived.

There were three builders in Indiana who built a majority of the covered bridges during the heyday of construction. J. J. Daniels of Rockville built about sixty covered bridges in Indiana. Most all of them were Burr Truss in type. He used vertical siding and wood shingles for the roof. Daniel's bridges were considered plain, using very little ornamentation.

Joseph A. Britton was also a native of Parke County and generally confined his work to Parke, Vermillion, and Putnam Counties. He built forty bridges during his career. Like those of Daniels, Britton's work was austere in design and used vertical siding and wood shingles for the roof. The three generations of the Kennedy family of Rushville built sixty very durable bridges primarily in Rush, Shelby, and adjoining counties. The Kennedy bridges are recognizable for their heavy durable Burr Arch construction, and for their graceful portals with elaborate woodwork.

The work of these three builders was evident during the busy middle period of covered bridge building days. Later on, when the large pine timbers were no longer easily available, and the iron bridges were becoming popular, the covered bridges that were built, were erected by local carpenters or lesser known companies.

That's enough of this humdrum historical and analytical treatise about covered bridges. Let's move on to the real excuse for even publishing this book—the mystique, the romance, and the sheer beauty of covered bridges as they gracefully augment the pastoral landscape of Indiana. The matchless imagery of the photographs of Marsha Williamson Mohr allow you to interject your own imagination into the story that these beautiful icons tell, limited only by the breadth of your own mind.

But first, we must settle one ever-present myth—why were the bridges ever covered in the first place? Let's have a little quiz. You can help solve that arguable piece of American folklore once and for all.

1. They were covered to prevent carriage and workhorses from being frightened by the depth of the riverbed, and by the noise of the flowing water.

2. Farmers could more easily drive herds of cattle, swine, sheep, and even turkeys through the closed structure.

3. It was a place for travelers to take shelter in the event of a sudden summer thunderstorm.

4. The dark interior of the bridge provided a secret place for lovers to steal a kiss.

5. The wide sides and portals of the bridges provided a visible place to hang circus posters, political handbills, and advertisements.

6. They were a good place to hold revivals, political rallies, and family reunions.

7. They added quiet beauty to their rural settings.

All of them are reasonable axioms and have their share of advocates, even among historians. Which one did you choose? Well, if you chose any of them, you are wrong. The real reason that those old bridges were covered was much less romantic, but more logical. They were covered to protect the vulnerable trusses, timbers, and floors from the damaging effects of rain, wind, snow, and rot. That's the simple truth. Sorry, because any of the others would have been much more fun.

The Essential Parts of a Good Bridge

A covered bridge is only as good as its foundation or abutments, and the strength of its framing or trusses.

The abutments or piers that support the bridge have a direct relationship to the parent material on which it rested. Basically, there is an abutment at each end of the bridge, and a pier at each end of each span. Single span bridges do not ordinarily have piers, but depend on the abutments for support. The material used for these foundations are an interesting study in the geology of the region. Wherever possible the stone was taken from the creek bed. Moving heavy stones long distances was avoided if at all possible. Limestone flagstones were the common material used in Indiana.

The trusses often were the trademarks of the builders, and they stridently expounded the values of their own design. Burr Arch and Howe Trusses were by far used the most in Indiana.

The early trusses were made from local timbers, either hewn or sawn, and generally were oak, poplar, or other species at hand. Later trusses were constructed of white pine from the northwoods, or yellow pine from the south.

Here are simple line drawings of trusses used in Indiana. None were typical. There were dozens of variations, depending on the particular use and the notions of the builders.

HOWE TRUSS: Easily fabricated off site using iron rods for strength, most of the bridges used the Howe Truss after 1880.

BURR ARCH: Handsome curved arches made of hewn or sawn timbers made this bridge easily identified. In later years these trusses were laminated and used for making longer spans, being by far the most common in Indiana bridges.

SMITH TRUSS: Largely prefabricated by Robert Smith in Toledo, Ohio, these trusses were light and strong. There are several versions of this truss.

The **LONG**, **QUEEN POST**, and **KING POST**, and other individually designed systems were rarely used.

Howe Truss

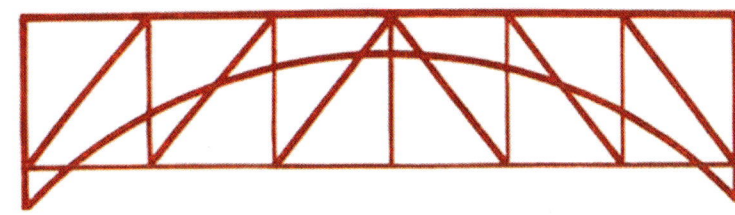

Burr Arch Truss

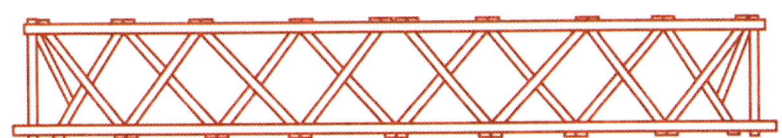

Smith type 4 Truss

Adams County

Adams County is a land of great ethnicity, settled largely by Swiss and Germans. They have carefully retained the traditions and the ethnics of their origin. They are people of conviction.

The large Amish population is well known as careful farmers, fine furniture craftsmen, and good carpenters. Their world is easily recognized for their "plain" way of life. Their simple dress, and their dependence on horses for farm work and transportation, testifies to their desire to avoid modern ways of living.

Adams County is a place of beautiful churches. Towering spires, particularly in the northern parts of the area, are spiritual centers for Catholics and Lutherans. The largest Mennonite Church in America is located in Berne. Other missionary congregations hold forth in beautiful modern churches.

The topography is level. The soils are dark, productive, and sometimes difficult to work, originating from heavy swamp parent materials. The famous Limberlost Swamp of Gene Stratton Porter fame occupied a large part of the southern part of the county. The agriculture is livestock oriented. There are many dairy herds in this county. They know the value of a life on the principle of hard work.

This area is a pleasant destination for travelers with its neat towns, striking farmsteads, and fine furniture stores. The roads are good and uncrowded. Watch for the buggies!

The Wabash River is fabled in Indiana folklore as the "highway" for Native Americans as they moved to new hunting grounds and traded with the French, English, and later American settlers. The Miami, Shawnee, Pottawattomie, and other tribes operated on or near the great river. The French established several forts on the Wabash for fur trading. Those forts were points of confrontation between the French, English, and later the Americans for control of the Northwest Territory.

However, in Adams County, this river was not mighty in any stretch of the imagination. It is quiet and tiny, originating just a few miles upstream, near Celina, Ohio.

The tiny Ceylon Bridge crosses the Wabash near Geneva, Indiana. It is the last of many bridges that spanned this river in earlier time.

Ceylon Bridge

Located five miles northeast of Geneva on County Road 950 South, the Ceylon Bridge is 126 feet long and was built in 1862. The construction is of Howe Truss design.

Bartholomew County

This county is a progressive place. Large and efficient farms and many new factories surround Columbus, often times called "The Athens of the Prairie" for its spectacular architecture.

Imaginative churches, wildly modernistic schools, banks with great looks, a wonderfully renovated courthouse, even a new shopping mall, all reflect the pride and the responsibility of the people in this great town. They have a world class Otter Creek Golf Course, and a covered bridge, moved into Mill Race Park and renovated completely.

One other small point. The Bartholomew County Historical Society has a very nice living history farm (the Breeding Farm) out north of Columbus. They have a fine Reeves steam traction engine and grain separator, both made in Columbus.

The New Brownsville Covered Bridge formerly spanned Clifty Creek about two miles east of Columbus. In 1966, it was moved to Mill Race Park in the city.

New Brownsville Bridge

Located in Mill Race Park in Columbus, the New Brownsville Bridge was built in 1840 and is 102 feet long. This is the only Long Truss bridge remaining in Indiana.

Brown County

Brown County, with its plethora of wooded hills, meandering streams, and glorious scenic overlooks, represents the beech and maple forest at their primeval best. Located only fifty miles south of Indianapolis, the wooded hills of this area are a mecca for tourists who somehow want to return to the simpler way of life. The annual trip to Brown County during the fall foliage season is a cherished event.

The huge Brown County State Park with its fine hiking trails, quiet lakes, abundant wildlife, and Abe Martin Lodge attracts outdoor enthusiasts who wish to renew their inner strength.

Quaint Nashville has carefully tended its attachment to the rustic past. Hundreds of craft and art shops, good eating places with biscuits and gravy, apple butter, country fried ham, and cherry pie is the perfect retreat for the hurried masses.

Any place with towns named Bean Blossom, Gnawbone, and Story deserve anyone's attention. Two covered bridges remain in the county. The Bean Blossom Bridge, hidden on a one-lane road two miles northwest of Bean Blossom stands in rural splendor there.

The Ramp Bridge is the only double-barreled structure in the state. It stood originally near Fincastle in Putnam County. It was moved to the north entrance of Brown County State Park in 1932 and undoubtedly is the heaviest traveled wooden bridge in the state.

Autumn in Brown County

Ramp Creek Bridge

Built in 1838 by Aaron Wolf, Ramp Creek Bridge is located at the main gate of Brown County State Park east of Nashville on Indiana State Road 46. The bridge is 60 feet long of double lane Burr Arch construction, and crosses Salt Creek.

Bean Blossom Bridge

Located two miles southwest of Bean Blossom and crossing Bean Blossom Creek, this bridge was built in 1880 and is 60 feet long. Construction was of modified Howe Truss.

Carroll County

People will tell you that Carroll County is representative of the flat productive Tipton Till plain of central Indiana. Crisscrossed by straight roads, it abounds in endless rows of tall corn and good soybeans, tied to the bright blue skies by tall silos, silver grain bins, and long hog barns. That's all true but it has a strange anomaly winding across its level terrain—Wildcat Creek. Sometimes troubled by industrial waste, soil runoff, and careless recreationists, it, nonetheless, retains its bucolic beauty.

The river was a godsend to early settlers with its wide and rich bottomland and easy access. It flowed deep and swift and supplied water for livestock, and was ideally suited to gristmills for grinding wheat for flour and corn for feed and food.

Fortunately, evidence of that early activity remains to this day. Modern farmers till the bottomland, encircled by huge sycamores, historic Adams Mill, and two fine covered bridges are still there, in fine condition.

Adams Mill is the tiny town of the same name about four miles east of Cutler on County Road 50 East. The mill is privately owned. You will need to inquire for the hours of operation. A few rods north of Adams Mill you will find their fine covered bridge. Heavily vandalized in years past, the bridge has been completely restored. It is a marvelous setting! Take your camera.

To get there, take County Road 500 South about five miles west to County Road 500 West. Turn south and you will find the red Lancaster Bridge over the Wildcat. It's well worth the trip!

Spring

Sense the first signs of warmth on your body
The wind puffing through your hair
Notice the traction on your palms as you drift with a kite
The first gust of tepid air through the windows

Heed the chirping of a Robin's revival
Consider the trickle of water after a spring rain

Smell the afresh revolution as the farmer plows
Lilacs from a startling distance

Sample the savory butter cooked mushrooms

Honor the blankets of Spring Beauties in the grass
Bees pollinating their territory
Vivid kites in the sky
Behold the beams of sunlight through the woods
as the sky opens after a shower
Watch the storms scheming from a far
Love the pastel colors of Easter eggs and fancy dresses
Examine the scattering of dandelion petals
The drift of clouds as you lull in the field

Spring is a time of renewal
A time of restoration
Of spiritual rebirth and expression

—Marsha Williamson Mohr

Summer

Feel the glow
The warmth of the sun's rays on your face
Sense the sand tickling your feet on the beach
The cool torrent as you spin in the waves
Touch the unblunted sticker bushes as you amble through the forest
Recognize the state of harmony inside you

Listen to the excitement of children on the playground
A smash of a bat on the ball field, the cheer of the rally
The Seagulls calling
Frogs croaking in a remote moor
Hear a bumblebee zipping

Smell the aroma of a cookout
Of newly mowed grass
Of wild roses blossoming in a grove

Taste the moisture of a good watermelon
Corn on the cob soaked with butter
Fresh strawberries with a touch of sweetener
Tomatoes with salt and pepper
Savor the refreshment of lemonade

See the rows and rows of bountiful crops
The wind blowing the grains of wheat
Visualize the butterflies dancing on the surface
Day Lilies in the channel
Fish vaulting on a line
Fireworks dancing in the nighttime
Behold the fluffy clouds as you unwind in the grass
Notice the bright colors of
The blue of the sky, the green of grass, the red of rural structures

Summer is a time of repose
An occasion for fellowship
An opening to make memories that last a lifetime

—Marsha Williamson Mohr

Autumn

Feel the suppressed leaves under your feet
The softness as you vault into a pile
Discover the heat on your expression as you roast a wiener on the fire
Manipulate the clammy strands amid a pumpkin as it begins to evolve

Listen to the sound of leaves crack as you shuffle through the woods
The waves of limber cornstalks blowing in the breeze
Hear the proclamation from a football field

Smell the fumes of burning fireplaces
The aroma of decayed leaves as you journey
The noteworthy scent of turkey cooking

Taste the spices of pumpkin pie
Of graham cracker, fire roasted marshmallows and melted chocolate

Take notice of the huge harvest moon as it settled on the horizon
The blending of magnificent hues of red, yellow, green and orange
Remember the bright leaves as they drift through the wind
And catch it if you can
Glimpse at the sunny red apples in a barrel
See people gathering at the flea market

Autumn is a time of anticipation
Anticipation of upcoming season
A time of gratitude
Of nature's lofty transition

—Marsha Williamson Mohr

Winter

Feel the sparkle of snowflakes on your face
The joy of silence
Explore the heaviness of your breathing as you walk through banks
The energy as the wind blows through your clothes
Feel the freedom of blades under you as you glide on the ice

Listen to the fireplace crackling
Children playing on the hills
Christmas Carols prepared in a church
Remember the quiet of winter
The hush of calmness

Smell the purity of a new snow
The simmer from chimneys

Taste the virtue of hot chocolate after a active day outside
The tart flavor of eggnog
Sugar cookies freshly baked

See the bright stars as they reach to touch you
The sunsets of brilliant comparison
View Christmas lights as they decorate the sky
Greens and red of holiday's spirits
Lavish the tiny tracks of animals surviving
Note the red, white and blue of a rural barn encompassed by new snow
and sapphire skies

Winter is a time of peace
Not hurried, not rushed
A cadence of family
A stage of settling back and taking a look
Of what life is about

—Marsha Williamson Mohr

Adams Mill, Cutler, Indiana

Adams Mill Bridge

The Worth of Age

Something new is:
Full of elegance
Focus for attention
Laden with dynamism
Self sufficient
Heavily photographed
Stands proud and functional

Something old is:
Less pleasing
Forsaken
With drudgery, needing labor
Costing assets to provide
Teeming of deformity
Unworthy to photograph
Ineligible to do the duty life has set out
for it to do

Life is like a covered bridge
Dawning with desire
If left ignored, ending with constraint
We need to give our love
Our love to all, immature or elderly
Functional, or not
To make them mindful
We are willing to secure measures
To preserve their distinction

—Marsha Williamson Mohr
West Lafayette, Indiana

Restoration/Adams Mill Bridge

Located five miles east of Cutler on County Road 50 East, Adams Mill Bridge was built of Howe Truss construction in 1872 by Wheelock Bridge Company. The bridge is 130 feet long.

Lancaster Bridge

From Cutler, take County Road 500 South west, following the Wildcat Creek valley to County Road 500 West. Turn south for two miles, and you will see it. Built of Howe Truss construction over the Wildcat Creek in 1872 by the Wheelock Bridge Company, this bridge is 133 feet in length and has cast iron abutments.

Dearborn County

The "slash lands" of southeastern Indiana is a unique area of the state that generally includes Franklin, Dearborn, Ohio, and Switzerland Counties. Geologically, it is made up of steep parallel hills primarily of shale and limestone substrata. Narrow valleys usually contain small rocky streams. The area is not suited to large-scale farming. The farms that do exist in this area are small livestock enterprises, often with tobacco growing allotments. The roads usually are steep and winding, following the hollows, and run in a northwest by southeast direction. It would appear that Dearborn County is trying to run off the map, right into the Ohio River.

Indiana Highway No. 1 is a very interesting road. If you want to take a tour sometime, follow that road from it's beginning in Lawrenceburg on the Ohio River all the way to Angola, near the Michigan line. You will pass through beautiful hilly lands at the south end, and pleasant farmlands, many small towns, a few cities, and the lake country to the north. If you're lucky, you can eat at Wellievers Smorgasbord in Hagerstown, one of the premier restaurants in the state.

At Guilford, in Dearborn County, a beautifully restored Kennedy bridge that has been moved to a roadside park on Highway 1 will surprise you.

Guilford Bridge

Built in 1879 by A. M. Kennedy and Sons of Burr Arch construction, this 119-foot-long bridge was strengthened in 1900 to carry heavy coal trucks. Also, this bridge is protected by a sprinkler system!

Decatur County

If you just like driving through wide-open countryside, Decatur County is the place. Big white barns and magnificent farms dominated the north half of the county. Then, as you drive south of Greensburg, you drift into gently rolling hills and towns like Millhousen, Smyrna, and Pinhook. (There's a good noisy place to eat in Millhousen.) Good German people there know how to live the good life! Five miles southeast of Westport, you will encounter what some say is the most beautiful covered bridge of them all, as it gracefully arches Sand Creek. This picturesque river valley provides a perfect setting for a perfect bridge. Notice the beautiful flagstone abutments. As is the case with most bridges, you can learn about the geological substrata of the land by studying the type of stone used for a foundation. They did not haul the heavy stone very far, but used what was close. This bridge has been bypassed so you can walk it all you wish. The full-length windows give you a great view of the creek. Before you leave the county, drive back to Greensburg and see the tree growing out of the courthouse dome, it's famous!

Westport Bridge

Located just southeast of Westport on 1100 South, Westport Bridge was built in 1880 of Burr Arch construction by A. M. Kennedy and Sons. This bridge crosses Sand Creek and is 131 feet long.

DeKalb County

Northern Indiana never had many covered bridges. The streams up there are rather slow and shallow and really didn't need a big complicated structure. Only one remains in DeKalb County. Go up there in the summertime. The weather is cool and the dairy farms are at their most photogenic. The red clover smells nice and red-winged blackbirds are everywhere.

Visit Auburn, at one time a famous automobile-manufacturing center. The Auburn Cord-Duesenberg Auto Museum, located in the old Cord factory, is well worth your visit. The annual antique auto auction is a delight, if you're rich enough to bid!

The St. Joseph's River is the only sizable stream in the county. The Spencerville Bridge crosses it on the southeast part of the county. You will find it is red and white, just like a bridge should look. Note the unusual sloping portals.

Spencerville Bridge

was built by George Woentz and Son in 1873 and is located just east of Spencerville on County Road 68. This Howe Truss constructed bridge has a single span and is 160 feet long.

Fayette County

The people in this fine old county cherish their own traditions and the land from whence they came.

Up in Posey Township, the great old houses and their pin-frame barns have been owned by generations of the same family and that fact will likely remain. Or, over around Alquina, big bank barns and substantial houses denote the families that live here who believe in the sanctity of the land and all that it produces.

The old Whitewater canal locks and excavations are still evident, if you know where to look. The Whitewater Valley Railroad slowly winds its way from Connersville to Metamora on summer weekends. The broad valley has more than its share of rural beauty for your enjoyment.

The typically ornate Longwood Bridge, built by the Kennedy brothers, formerly crossed Williams Creek in western Fayette County. It is another example of the lucky few that went to covered bridge heaven—a public park. This fine structure was dismantled and moved to busy Roberts Park on Highway 1 in Connersville. While you're there, walk over to the old fairgrounds harness horse track. That will take you back to the golden age of county fairs!

Longwood Bridge

Built by the Kennedy Brothers (can't you tell) in 1884 of Burr Arch construction, the Longwood Bridge is 108 feet long.

Fountain County

This spacious county is a pleasant mixture of broad prairies, the Wabash River and the small streams that rush toward their demise disappearing into the river with a swirl of silt and debris, and several streams that wind their way southward, everyone of them a prime target for a covered bridge. You should visit the county courthouse at Covington where the interior walls are covered by magnificent murals, painted by unemployed artists during the Great Depression of the 1930s. The Portland Arch Nature Preserve near the Wabash River in northern Fountain County, is a place of peaceful solitude. See it.

There are three covered bridges that are in a natural state of good repair, sitting unadorned in the countryside at its natural best. No fixing up for tourists here. Oddly, all three bridges are similar in appearance, and built at about the same time by some obscure and unknown builder. Fountain County is just like its three bridges. They are what they are, and nothing more.

Rob Roy Bridge (left)

The Rob Roy Bridge crosses Big Shawnee Creek north of Rob Roy just off U.S. 41. Built in 1860 of Howe Truss construction, this bridge is 105 feet in length.

Cades Mill Bridge (above)

Cades Mill Bridge is located six miles southwest of Veedersburg off County Road 300 West on County Road 420 South. Built of Howe Truss construction in 1854, this bridge crosses Coal Creek and is 150 feet long.

Wallace Bridge (opposite bottom)

Built in 1871 of Howe Truss construction, the Wallace Bridge crosses Sugar Mill Creek and is located on the southeast edge of Wallace on County Road 1000 south. (Oddly, all three of these bridges, the Rob Roy, Cades Mill Bridge, and Wallace Bridge, are similar in appearance and built at about the same time by some obscure and unknown builder.)

Franklin County

I'll guarantee you one thing: if you'll drive Indiana 121 from Connersville, down the East Fork of the Whitewater River, through Alpine and Laurel to U.S. 52 and over to Metamora during the height of the red bud season, you will agree with me that Franklin County is one of the most delightful areas in all of Indiana. The steep hills are absolutely bursting with the fuchsia bloom of that woodland tree. Mixed with the light green of the new leaves of the maple, ash, and sassafras, the awakening of spring is a tonic for the soul. Take the time to walk the little streets of Metamora. Visit the shops and eat in some little cafe. Enjoy the restored mill and be amazed with the aqueduct that carries the Whitewater Canal over Duck Creek.

Then go on over to Brookville and see the magnificent old homes and the Victorian business center. Go back through Metamora to the Peppertown Road (Indiana 229), and head south to Oldenburg on 600 South, jog south to 640 South and on over to the Stockheighter Bridge. Drive further south to Batesville and eat some great German food in the Sherman House. And there's much more. The huge Brookville Lake and its many great views will invite you back for some great striped bass fishing in the summer. You won't want to leave.

Whitewater Canal Aqueduct

The only aqueduct covered bridge in America is located in Metamora, ten miles west of Brookville on U.S. 52. Built in 1846 of Burr Arch construction and restored in 1991, Whitewater Canal Aqueduct carries Whitewater Canal over Duck Creek and is 60 feet long.

Seal Barn Bridge

This bridge is located on private property north of Cedar Grove on Big Cedar Road. A combination bridge and barn of Queen Post construction, Seal Barn Bridge was built in 1905 and is 56 feet in length.

Snow Hill Bridge

Spanning Johnson's Creek, Snow Hill Bridge is located two miles north of Rockdale on Johnson Fork Road. Built in 1894 of Howe Truss design, this bridge is 84 feet long.

Stockheughter Bridge

Built in 1887 of Howe Truss construction, Stockheughter Bridge is located east of Enochsburg on County Road 640 South. This bridge is 92 feet in length and crosses Salt Creek.

Gibson County

When you cross the big White River south of Vincennes on U.S. 41, you can feel just a touch of the South. Cypress swamps begin to show up in depressed areas along the White and Wabash Rivers. The deep rich brown of the unpainted cypress-sided barns blend so nicely with the tan sandy loams of the bottoms. West of Princeton, the burning gases of the oil wells light your way. The oil well pumps, standing like storks over their precious resource, make farming a whole lot more profitable. The highlands to the east still belch forth coal, fuel for the power plants on the White, Wabash, and Ohio Rivers. Gibson County is rich in its natural resources and now, the huge Toyota truck plant adds to its value.

Wheeling Bridge

Located over the Patoka River seven miles north of Princeton on Indiana 65, turn east on County Road 400 North, jog south, and then back east. Built by William T. Washer of Smith No. 4 trusses in 1877, this bridge is 163 feet long and is on the edge of Patoka River National Wildlife Reserve.

Old Red

A fitting name for a venerable old bridge: remote and hard to find. Built in 1875 of Smith No. 4 construction, this bridge is 170 feet in length. Old Red is located four miles south of Crawleyville to the west of 1675 West, crossing Big Bayou Creek.

Grant County

Grant County has much to offer. Large and efficient corn, soybean, and swine farms dominate the western half of the county. Marion, the county seat, is an energetic manufacturing town. Fairmount was the boyhood home of Hollywood legend James Dean. He is buried there and there is a fine museum in his honor.

Van Buren brags of its Weaver Popcorn Company, one of the country's largest. The first of the really small cars, the Crosley, was built in Marion. The natural gas boom of the 1890s brought many glass factories to eastern Indiana. Grant County shared in that short-lived prosperity.

Matthews, in the far southwestern part of the county, is so proud of its Cumberland covered bridge over the Mississinawa River, that it holds a big festival in its behalf every fall, in the park adjacent to the bridge.

Cumberland Bridge

Built of Howe Truss construction by the Smith Bridge Company in 1877, this bridge is 175 feet long and is located on Second Street, just east of Matthews. Cumberland Bridge was returned to its original site after it was washed away in the 1913 flood.

Greene County

Greene County is a rich land of broad and varied plains separated by rolling ridges. The wide White River Valley on the west side is good farming ground. The eastern half of this scenic land is a widely undulating tumble of sassafras, hickory, poplar, and oak trees with small hill farms and

rural residences scattered in between. The western border is dominated by old strip mines, the center by the White River Valley, and the east is sharp unglaciated hills and deep valleys. Don't miss the high railroad trestle at Tulip!

Some covered bridges seem to clash with the environment around them. Such is not the case with the Richland-Plummer Creek Bridge south of Bloomfield. This delicate Kennedy bridge framed by red bud, beech, and maples paints a perfect picture of the pleasant intertwining of the beauty of nature and the sensitivity of an artist at work. Once near ruin, this bridge has been restored to its original state.

Richland-Plummer Creek Bridge

Richland-Plummer Creek Bridge is located three miles south of Bloomfield on U.S. 231 to County Road 175. Turn west to County Road 25 East, then south for one and a half miles. Built by A. M. Kennedy and Sons of Burr Arch construction and completed originally in 1883, this bridge spans 119 feet.

Hamilton County

Upscale housing developments dominate the south half of this county, a close neighbor of Indianapolis, while the northern half retains its rural agricultural setting. Careful attention to tasteful growth is the trademark of this burgeoning area. Highly developed Geist and Morse reservoirs and the scenic opportunities near the White River add to the quality of life in Hamilton County. There are also delightful small towns like Cicero, Arcadia, Atlanta, and Sheridan if you like a slower pace.

Conner Prairie Settlement is one of the nations premier living history museums. Recently they moved and restored the spectacular Cedar Chapel Bridge (a pretty name) from DeKalb County. You will need to pay admission to see the museum and bridge, but it is well worth it.

Potter's Bridge over the White River is a large and beautiful sight. It's north of Noblesville.

Potter's Bridge
(opposite)
Potter's Bridge was built in 1871 and rebuilt in 1937. It is located on Allisonville Road, three miles north of Noblesville. Originally built by Josiah Durfee of Howe Truss construction, the twin-spanned bridge is 259 feet long.

Cedar Chapel Bridge
(above)
Cedar Chapel Bridge was built in 1884 in DeKalb County of Howe Truss design and is located as part of the Conner Prairie Settlement on Allisonville Road, four miles south of Noblesville. This bridge is 110 feet in length. Note roof cupolas and viewing windows.

Howard County

Howard County is a rich agricultural county of mostly Class I lands, and a wonderland for modern farmers. Only one sizable stream, the Wildcat, traverses the county, and it had one covered bridge, about five miles east of Kokomo, that was moldering away, and destined to be destroyed by modern heavy traffic. In 1958, it was dismantled and moved to Highland Park in Kokomo. Such has been, thankfully, the fate of many bridges that stand in the way of progress. They will be enjoyed by generations to come.

Kokomo is an industrial town with several large plants manufacturing automobile components. That is not a recent development. The Haynes car was the first operational automobile in America. It was built in Kokomo and test driven on Pumpkinvine Pike on the eastside of town.

Vermont Bridge

Erected in 1875 and moved in 1959 to Highland Park in southwest Kokomo, the Vermont Bridge is 98 feet long and was constructed of Modified Smith Truss.

Jackson County

The East Fork of the White River heavily influences this good farming community. Its sandy bottoms raise beautiful crops of watermelon, cantaloupe, and sweet corn. Watch for roadside stands around Brownstown and Villonia.

If you're around Brownstown in July, visit their county fair. It will take you back to the happy days of your youth. Life is good down there.

Three very long covered bridges gracefully span the broad White River. All are easily reached and sit in relative solitude, waiting for you to visit. They may be closed to vehicular traffic, but you can walk their long lengths. Notice the beautiful limestone abutments.

Bells Ford Bridge

Located on Indiana 256 two miles northwest of Seymour, Bells Ford Bridge is closed to car traffic. Built by Seymour Bridge Company of Post Truss construction in 1875, the twin span bridge is the only Post Truss bridge in the world.

Shieldstone Bridge

Built by J. J. Daniels of Burr Arch Truss in 1876, Shieldstown Bridge is 231 feet long and is located three and one-half miles east of Brownstown on U.S. 50, then north one mile on unmarked Shields Road.

Medora Bridge

Medora Bridge is the longest existing covered bridge in the United States. Also built by J. J. Daniels, this bridge has three spans of Burr Truss construction, and is 458 feet long. Located two miles east of Medora on Indiana 235.

Jennings County

Jennings County is a pleasant rural county dissected southwesterly by tumbling streams hurrying through wooded, deep valleys; Sand Creek, the Muscatatuck, and Graham Creek, to name a few. Interspersed with the woodlands and the small farms are several fish and wildlife areas and nature preserves. The huge Crosley Fish and Wildlife Area provides a quiet place to get back to nature and offers fine fishing and hunting in season.

The northern half of the county is dotted with housing developments for folks working in industrial Columbus, seeking a more peaceful surrounding.

Two fine covered bridges, James and Scipio, are restored and sit in rustic splendor for your enjoyment.

Visit little Vernon, their county seat. Walk around the courthouse square. Things are very much as they always were.

Scipio Bridge
(above and top right)

Scipio Bridge was built in 1886 of Howe Truss design and is 124 feet in length. The actual builder is questionable and the bridge was moved from an unknown location. Crossing Sand Creek, this bridge is located on the north edge of Scipio just off Indiana 7.

James Bridge
(opposite bottom)

Constructed in 1887 over Graham Creek by Baron & Hole, the length of this bridge is 124 feet. Constructed of Howe Truss design, the James Bridge is located five miles south of Vernon on Indiana 3, east on County Road 650 South.

WEIGHT
LIMIT
11
TONS

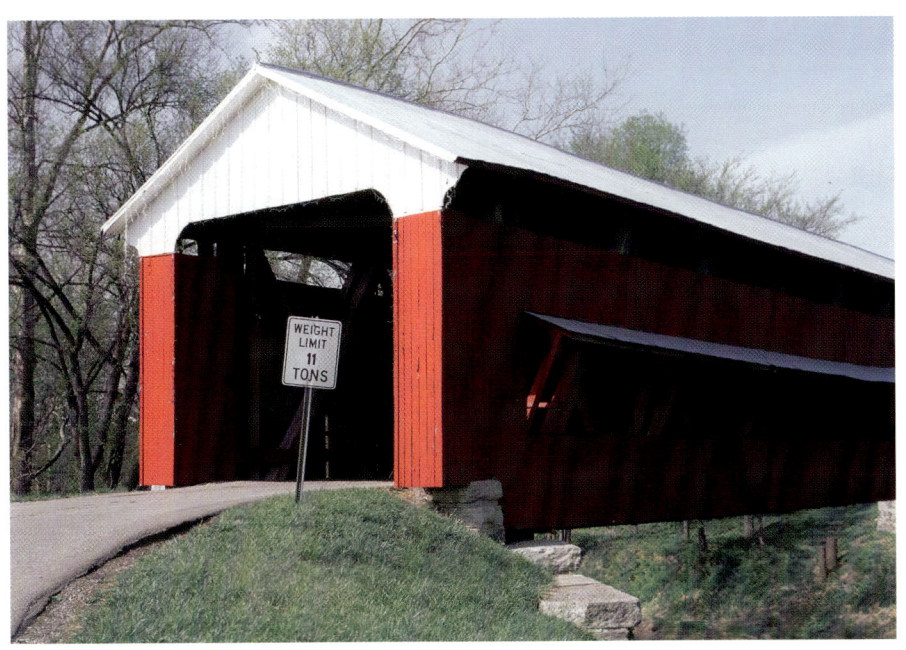

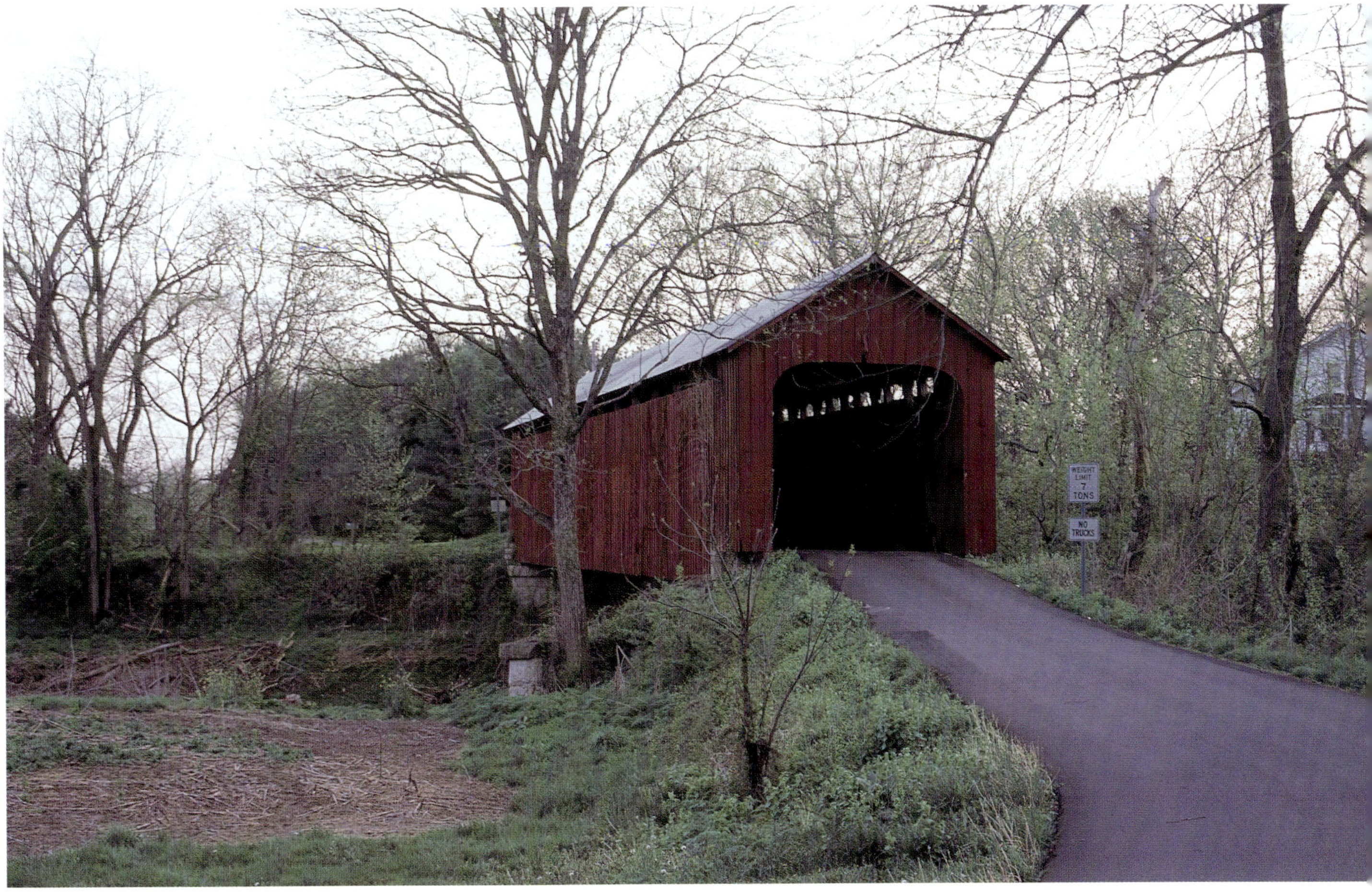
WEIGHT
LIMIT
7
TONS
NO
TRUCKS

Lake County

Lake County, Indiana, a clashing cacophony of cultures, nationalities, occupations, and environments, dramatically depicts the strengths of people who rise above their inherent differences to meld into a society that is for the common good.

In an area seemingly filled with the trappings of human encroachment, careful attention to nature, history, and beauty is apparent. The roar of the highways, the stench of steel mills and refineries, and the rush of humanity cannot quench the peace of Lake Michigan as it washes over the beautiful beaches and dunes of its peaceful shore. Nor has the great Kankakee Swamp been obliterated. The shallow ponds, the moldering hunting lodges, and the black oak hummocks remain, ready for organizations to restore the old Kankakee River to some of its original glory. Habitat restoration for herons, rails, duck, geese, and maybe even prairie chickens, is now under way and holds great promise for future generations.

But, for all those good things, Lake County did not have a single covered bridge. Being the determined people they are, they just moved in a bridge, lock, stock, and barrel from Rush County. It now presides in the county fairgrounds in Crown Point.

Fairgrounds Bridge

Moved from Milroy, Indiana, in 1933, Fairgrounds Bridge is now located in the county fairgrounds, Court Street, Crown Point. Originally built by A. M. Kennedy and Sons of Burr Arch design, this bridge spans 101 feet in length.

Lawrence County

Lawrence County is limestone country. The quarries there (and Monroe County to the north), supply a majority of America's fine building stone. The Empire State Building, the Pentagon, and many other government sites show the mark of the Hoosier state. Drive through any deep cut in the county and you will appreciate the character of this beautiful building material.

Limestone's base material makes for rich soil, and rich limestone soils grow lush pastures. Lawrence County is cattle land range, and they make good use of those beautiful grazing lands. Drive any county road and you will see firsthand tall beech, maple, and poplar trees, home for wild turkey, deer, and raccoons.

If you have the time, meander down Indiana 450 through the hills and dales of the White River Valley. Take a picture of the old Williams flour mill, still operating as a feed elevator. Stop for a spell. It's a wonderful place to loaf and catch up on the news. A few miles down the road you will see Williams Bridge, all 376 feet of it! The longest covered bridge in Indiana still open to traffic. Stay on Indiana 450 all the way to Shoals. It's very crooked and very beautiful!

Williams Bridge

Located one mile west of Williams on Indiana 450, south on County Road 1000 West, this bridge was probably built by J. J. Daniels in 1884 of Howe Truss construction. Williams Bridge has two spans, each 376 feet in length, and was restored in 1985. If you like graffiti, this is the place!

Marion County

Surprisingly, Marion County had many covered bridges in times past. Probably the most well known was the National Road Bridge over the White River. It was broad with two-way traffic and a pedestrian path on both sides. Lavishly appointed with colonnaded entrances, it suffered from general neglect and the damaging effects of thousands of heavy freight wagons rumbling carelessly through it for seventy-two years. It was aesthetically ruined by being covered, inside and out, by billboards, placards, and posters from one end to the other. To add insult to injury, the bridge became a haven for bums, drunks, and unsavory characters. It was a thoroughly unsafe place to be. Mercifully in 1907, it was demolished.

Now, only one bridge remains in the county. Traders Point Bridge crossed Fishback Creek on the northwest side on Eighty-sixth Street. In 1960 it was purchased and moved to a private estate on the northwest side.

There is much to be seen in Indianapolis. Many fine museums, the Children's Museum, The Indianapolis Museum of Art, and the Eiteljorg, to name a few. The Indiana State Fair, with its incomparable Pioneer Village, runs for two weeks every August. By all means, visit White River State Park and Zoo on the near Westside.

Traders Point Bridge

Built by Josiah Durfee in 1876, Traders Point Bridge was moved to a private estate in 1960. Constructed of Howe Truss design, this bridge is 88 feet long.

Montgomery County

There is much that can be said about this west central Indiana county. It is one of the leading agricultural areas in the state, with many exciting country drives. Crawfordsville, the county seat, is architecturally a wonder. The courthouse square is filled with great shops. Wabash College is a prestigious institution with a beautiful campus near downtown. But for anyone who enjoys streams that offer generous portions of scenic beauty, Sugar Creek is the one. A popular canoe creek, the high limestone bluffs, the wooded banks, and the rippling current is incomparable. There were, at one time, several covered bridges spanning this creek. Now only two remain. But you now have this great collection of color pictures of a fantastic stream and its environs.

Whatever you do, visit Shades State Park on Sugar Creek in the western part of the county. Not many improvements here and that's the best part of it.

The Bluffs of Sugar Creek

Darlington Bridge

Darlington Bridge is located on Cassidy Road at the west edge of Darlington. Built in 1868 by Joseph Kress of Howe Truss design, this bridge has two spans and is 166 feet in length.

Deer's Mill Bridge

Built by J. J. Daniels in 1878 of Burr Arch Truss design, Deer's Mills Bridge is located on Indiana 234. This colorful trademark of Shades State Park has two spans over a deep chasm and is 275 feet long.

Owen County

When you head south of Cloverdale on U.S. 231 and mounds of wooded hills appear ahead of you, you know you have reached "Sweet Owen County." The land of sausage and biscuits, apple cider, old-fashioned family reunions, and all night coon hunts. Somehow, the little farms with a few sheep, a patch of corn, a good pickup truck, and a fine job in town, bring a spirit of independence. And the nature of things aided and abetted that attitude. The woods, good fishing rivers, and rushing cataracts, made the living good. Every little town had a fine grocery store with a gas pump out front. All is well! Sadly perhaps, the folks living in the rush of big city life discovered that it wasn't such a bad idea. They bought a piece of ground, built a log cabin, and settled in for the good life. That's alright, the natives said. There's enough room in "Sweet Owen County" for everyone.

The East Fork of the White River dissects the county and required wooden or iron bridges to cross that broad stream. Sadly, all the covered bridges on White River are gone. The only remaining bridge in the county is the supremely beautiful Cataract Falls Bridge over the headwaters of Cagles Mill Lake. It's a must see!

Cataract Falls

Crossing Mill Creek, Cataract Falls is located six miles south of Cloverdale on U.S. 231, west of 105 North.

Cataract Falls Bridge

Cataract Falls Bridge was built in 1876 of Modified Smith Truss design, and is 140 feet long. The extensive scenic area where it is located is known as the Richard Lieber Park and Cataract Falls States Recreation Area.

Parke County

When you get right down to it, Parke County is what this nice book is all about: a veritable paradise of wooded hills, delightful country roads, and many rivers and streams rippling through limestone-lined bluffs. Parke County has more covered bridges than most states and about a third of the structures in Indiana.

The great number of covered bridges in Parke County might be attributed to the incidence of substantial rivers and streams with high banks that need strong bridges. Or, more likely, it is the fact that two of the most prolific bridge builders, J. J. Daniels and the Britton family, lived and worked in Parke County.

I suggest that you carefully plan your route to see all the bridges, mills, and pretty country. Go to the Parke County, Inc. office in the old railroad depot in Rockville. They have maps and planned routes for your use.

In addition to touring Parke County to enjoy the countryside and the magnificent covered bridges, there is much more for you to do.

The huge Covered Bridge Festival is held for about ten days in October. The whole county comes alive with music and food, crafts and demonstrations of all sorts, and special bus tours of all the covered bridges. It's amazing!

The Maple Syrup Festival is another joyous occasion. When the maple sap is running and the maple sugar camps are in action, you must join in the fun. This festival is held in March of each year.

For information on these festivals and other attractions in Parke County, write or call Parke County, Inc., P.O. box 165, Rockville, Indiana 47872, (765-569-5226).

You certainly should visit Billie Creek Village just east of Rockville on U.S. 36. Here you can stroll through those good old days of quaint farms, quiet little towns and, of course, covered bridges. There is a good resort motel and restaurant on the grounds. They also have several special events during the year such as "threshing days," "maple sugar days," and many more. It's a wonderful place.

Food, Fun, and Covered Bridges

Many small towns in Parke County join in the fun during the Covered Bridge Festival. Bridgeton, with its beautiful bridge and mill, turns into a real art colony for those special days.

For your reference, I have grouped the bridges more or less by geographic area from north to south. Don't try to see them all by just driving around. Get the maps and routes from the festival office and follow them methodically. Consider what we have here to be merely an artistic overview of these beautiful and historic structures.

Parke County, Indiana
The Beauty of Parke County

A country road.

Spring (above) Fall (below)

The Seasons on Sugar Creek

Summer (above) Winter (below)

The Bridges of Northeastern Parke County
The Narrows

This is probably the most photographed bridge in Indiana and is located on County Road 375 East on the east edge of Turkey Run State Park, crossing a rocky gorge of Sugar Creek. Built by J. A. Britton in 1882 of Burr Arch Truss design, Narrows Bridge is 121 feet in length.

Wilkins Mill Bridge

Located near U.S. 41, just northwest of Turkey Run Park over the dry bed of Sugar Mill Creek, Wilkins Mill Bridge was built in 1906 by William Hendricks and is of Burr Arch construction. Being isolated and very hard to find, visitors must ford a relocated creek at both ends to reach this covered bridge.

Cox Ford Bridge

Built in 1913 by J. A. Britton to replace an iron bridge washed out in the great 1913 flood, Cox Ford Bridge is 176 feet long of double Burr Arch construction, and is located in a beautiful wooded area. It is located at the west edge of Turkey Run Park over Sugar Creek.

The Bridges of Northwest Parke County
Bowsher Ford Bridge

Constructed of Burr Arch design, this bridge has a 72-foot span and was built in 1915 by Eugene Britton. Bowsher Ford Bridge is located west of Tangier on County Road 1050 North, cross Mill Creek, and then turn north for one mile.

Jackson Bridge

This beautiful white bridge, located on County Road 775 North and County Road 50 West out of Bloomingdale and Annapolis, crosses Sugar Creek and has the longest single span, double Burr Arch design still in use (207 feet long). Built in 1861 by J. J. Daniels.

Rush Creek Bridge (top)

This picture perfect bridge in a wooded setting is located south of Tangier. Take County Road 450 West, turn east on County Road 900 North, and there you are! With its cut stone abutments and its Burr Arch construction, this bridge was built by William Hendricks in 1904, is 77 feet in length, and crosses the tiny creek by the same name.

Mill Creek-Tow Path Bridge (bottom)

You will have to follow our directions west of Tangier on 1050 North to Mill Creek then turn south for one-half mile as this bridge is not on the tour route because of its isolated location. Located near the old Erie Canal, Mill Creek-Tow Path Bridge was built in 1907 by William Hendricks of Burr Arch construction, and is 92 feet long.

Corner Café

Larry and I were bicycling, once again, the beautiful countryside of Parke County, Indiana. In the small town of Marshall, they have a nice café where we have eaten several times before. We recognized this would be a nice stopping point for our trip.

A little lady, ambulating with assistance of a walker, was exiting the café. Larry voiced a pleasant greeting. She kindly responded. The greeting ended up being a lengthy conversation.

It was a pleasant visit. We shared several subjects. One subject being my upcoming article on the covered bridges in Country Magazine. She voiced her love for these bridges, living in Parke County all her life. I especially liked the story about the family outings at the covered bridges. She continued to tell us about how her father built several of the trestles. Larry and I greatly enjoyed our chat.

She exited the café, only to return. It was difficult for her to open both doors and maneuver the walker. On her return, she stated which house was hers, "The one with the cows in front," and to come visit anytime. We both questioned the cows? Will they still be standing in front? How kind.

The article came out in December. We ordered extra copies of the magazine. On one very cold January day, Larry and I again returned to Parke County to share the essay with several people of this area whom we were blessed with their acquaintance.

It was obvious which home was our little Corner Café Lady's. The cows were cement, but of course. I knocked and knocked. It was bitterly cold. "Please answer," I said over and over to myself. No answer. We were so disappointed. I hoped, we hoped, she would perhaps see the article sometime. Pausing in her driveway, we also hoped she was in good health.

—Marsha Williamson Mohr

Marshall Bridge

Joseph Britton built this new 56-foot-long bridge of Burr Arch construction when he was eighty years of age. Crossing Rush Creek, this bridge is located three miles south of Tangier on County Road 800 North at County Road 450 West in a heavily wooded, deep valley. There are six covered bridges within a five-mile radius of Tangier—surely a treasure trove of history.

The Bridges of East Central Parke County
The Neet Bridge

Crossing Little Raccoon Creek, this bridge is located three miles south of Rockville on County Road 200 East. The last bridge built by J. J. Daniels in 1904, Neet Bridge is of Burr Arch construction, and is 143 feet in length. The setting is typical of many bridges in this county, a broad valley, and a good view.

The Nevins Bridge

Originally built at Caitlin and constructed of Burr Arch design, Nevins Bridge is 155 feet long and it is NOT red. Located five miles south of Rockville on County Road 130 East on the Little Raccoon Creek, this bridge represents the end of an era—Parke County's last bridge and the last bridge built by Joseph Britton in 1920.

McAllister Bridge

Built by Joseph A. Britton in 1914 of Burr Arch construction, this single span over the Little Raccoon Creek is 122 feet in length. Located two miles south of Rockville on County Road 200 East then east on County Road 400 south. Notice many of the later bridges had concrete foundations and the road was raised to avoid high water.

Spring (above) Fall (below)

The Seasons at McAllister Bridge

102

Summer (above) Winter (below)

103

Crooks Bridge

Crossing the Little Raccoon Creek on County Road 225 East to County Road 300 South (two miles southeast of Rockville), this is the oldest covered bridge in the county. Built in 1856, Crooks Bridge lay abandoned for many years before reconstruction at the present site after the road was closed. Constructed of double Burr Arch design, this bridge was erected on hand-hewn stone abutments by Henry Wolfe.

Billie Creek Bridge

Located at Billie Creek Village east of Rockville, this bridge crosses Williams Creek, hence the name "Billie." Built in 1895 of Burr Arch construction by J. J. Daniels, Billie Creek Bridge is 62 feet long.

Beeson Bridge (top)
Now crossing Williams Creek at the entrance to Billie Creek Village, this bridge was originally on Roaring Creek near Marshall. Built in 1906 by Frankfort Construction Company of Burr Arch construction, Beeson Bridge is 55 feet long, and was moved to its present site in 1980.

Leatherwood Station Bridge (bottom)
Originally spanning Leather Creek west of Rockville, Leatherwood Station Bridge is now located on a beautiful wooded site in Billie Creek Village, but you must take the wagon tour to see this one. Built by Joseph Britton in 1899 of Burr Arch construction, all 72 feet of this bridge was moved to its new site in 1981.

Mansfield Bridge and Mill

The Mansfield Roller Mill, 1880.

The Visual

As I sit, gaze and marvel
Sit in the doorway of a covered bridge
A one lane gravel road
One tree perfectly arranged on that road
The hills in the distance
The rows of crops
Stand back, and notice the old wooden structure framing the scene
Like a photograph
Waiting to be captured

Looking out as I stand at a window of the covered bridge
I hear the trickle of the water beneath me
I see the mill through the opening
The waterfall to it's side
What a wonderful sight
Stand back, and notice the old wooden structure framing the scene
Like a photograph
Waiting to be captured

Think as I may, what a beautiful sight
A sight I think I will just enjoy this time
This time it's for only me

—Marsha Williamson Mohr

This bridge is located on Indiana 59 in the small town of Mansfield and crosses Big Raccoon Creek. Built in 1867 by Joseph J. Daniels, the twin span Burr Arch design is 247 feet long. (Most covered bridges were built near water-powered mills, little towns, or some local industry. Many times they crossed rivers at a ford or other feature that made it easy for construction. May have been named after a local farmer, politician, or a hero.)

People of Parke County

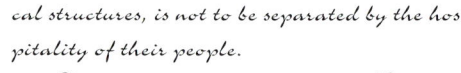

Parke County, Indiana, hosts the largest number of covered bridges than any other county in the United States. The rolling hills, the gentle terrain, the rural historical structures, is not to be separated by the hospitality of their people.

One favorite activity of ours in Parke County is bicycling. The slow speed of the vehicle helps one perpetuate the scenes. Few and far between is civilization. Frequently seen, however, are the covered bridges.

Our first bicycling adventure, Larry and I decided to stop in the little town of Mansfield. This town has a covered bridge and a gristmill. What a beautiful sight it was. What beautiful sounds the small waterfall at the mill's edge made. I especially adore viewing the mill from the covered bridge's window; it is one of my all time favorite scenes. We had the notion to have lunch sitting beside the waterfall viewing both the mill and the bridge.

Off-season not much is going on, especially during the week. We noticed three people sitting on a bench outside a little store. No other cars, no other humanity. After a pleasant greeting, "If you need anything let me know," Larry and I entered the store. Nothing but pop and chips. Walking back outside I asked, "Do you have anything a little more substantial?" "Mrs. Smith on the corner has sandwiches, but just on weekends. Well, I do have a chicken cooking out back, one hamburger bun and hopefully one hot dog bun, someone will have to eat their barbecue on a hot dog instead of hamburger bun, and I think I have a half a bag of chips. If you want to come back in about 20 minutes, I will have lunch for you." Tammy Dover responded. "Great, thank you very much," we both replied.

In twenty minutes, Larry and I walked back into the store. Carefully prepared were the sandwiches and compliments. Being uncertain what to charge for the lunch, Tammy paused. Larry graciously paid more than what she reluctantly requested.

Our lunch was phenomenal. As we ate, we watched two young boys dressed in suspenders fishing in the water below the falls. What a scene. A covered bridge on one side, and the mill on the other. One would have to marvel, what could be a better way to spend lunch. One would have to marvel, where kinder people could be found.

—Marsha Williamson Mohr

Portland Mills Bridge

This bridge is located south of Waveland on Indiana 59 (about two miles) and then west on County Road 650 North.

Spring (above) Fall (below)

The Seasons of Portland Mills Bridge

Portland Mills Bridge, built by Henry Wolfe in 1856, was formerly located in the small town of Portland Mills and moved to its present location in

Summer (above) Winter (below)

1960. Crossing the Little Raccoon Creek for 131 feet, this bridge structure has horizontal drop siding, unusual except for Kennedy bridges, and is of Burr Arch construction.

Sanatorium Bridge

Built in 1913 by Joseph A. Britton of Burr Arch Truss design, this bridge spans the Little Raccoon Creek for 154 feet and was constructed by the Tuberculosis Sanatorium to haul coal to its power plant. Sanatorium Bridge is located on private property, two miles east of Rockville on U.S. 36 on a very hard to find, very rough road.

The Bridges of West Central Parke County

West Union Bridge (opposite)

Located on County Road 525 West, one mile north of West Union, on Sugar Creek near its confluence with the Wabash. The third covered bridge on this location was built in 1876 by Joseph J. Daniels as a two span, double Burr Arch. This is the longest bridge in the county at 315 feet and was constructed on a beautiful stone foundation. West Union Bridge has been bypassed for vehicles, so it is a beautiful spot for a picnic and a nice leisurely walk across to the other side.

115

Melcher Bridge

This pretty bridge in a wooded setting is located two miles east of Montezuma on County Road 45 past the little town of Klondyke where it crosses the Leatherwood Creek. Constructed of Burr Arch design by Joseph J. Daniels in 1896, this bridge is 83 feet long.

Sim Smith Bridge (opposite)

Joseph A. Britton built this tiny bridge, all 84 feet of it, of Burr Arch construction in 1883 on fine sandstone abutments. Located over Leatherwood Creek two miles east of Montezuma on County Road 40 North at County Road 310 West. Be very careful when you visit because this bridge is haunted. If you hear a horse and buggy, run for your life!

Rolling rural Parke County, Indiana, with it's thirty-two covered bridges, offers homage in each season.

In spring:
I see brilliant rose Redbud trees contrasting the white and ruby bridges
Gleaming fair green trees on the hilltops
May Apples adjacent the roadway
Mud puddles on gravel routes
Robins gathering worms
Spreading water levels beneath the bridges
Sapphire skies praising the pastel tones

In summer:
I see orange Day Lilies and yellow Black-eyed Susans near the bridges
Comely dark green trees in the grove
Children playing in the water underneath
Adults canoeing
Corn growing tall in fields, exhibiting fitness
Grasshoppers jumping
Woolly worms crossing the track
Velvety clouds confronting the turquoise sky

In autumn:
I see lucent fusion of orange, yellow, red and green honoring the tinge of the ruby bridges
Blanket of leaves covering the soil
Reflective ponds
Pumpkins adorning front porches
Autumn displays in yards
Leaves afloat the supple waters
The gentle lighting of overcast skies inflate the golden hues of autumn

In winter:
I see patriotic red, white and blue tones of the bridge, fresh snow and bright royal skies
Steam rising from polar creeks
Frosty ice fabrications
Ducks rescuing the final unfrozen section on the pellucid waters
Yuletide lights trimming buildings
Wreaths clothing doorways
Silhouettes on snowfall from nigh hardwood
Gleaming winter skies prolific with aspen glow, declaring an end of another day
Another day overflowing with the gladness of changeful climates

—Marsha Williamson Mohr

Phillips or Arabia Bridge

Rather than involve you in a host of details, I want you to sit back and enjoy the photographic genius of Marsha Williamson Mohr, as she captures the pastoral beauty of this tiny bridge. Located just off U.S. 36, five miles west of Rockville.

Mecca Bridge (top)

Built by Joseph J. Daniels in 1873 of Burr Arch, single-span design, this bridge is 150 feet in length. Crossing Big Raccoon Creek, Mecca Bridge is located on the east edge of Mecca on County road 136. A restored one-room school is its neighbor.

Caitlin Bridge (bottom)

Built in 1907 by Clark McDaniel near Catlin, this bridge of Burr Arch design is 54 feet in length and is located on the golf course north of Rockville on U.S. 41. Park on the golf course and walk to the bridge. Catlin Bridge was in total disrepair and condemned in the original location, but was moved to its present location in 1961. No golf today!

Zacke Cox Bridge

Named for a prominent landowner in the community, Zacke Cox Bridge crosses Rock Run Creek on County Road 325 West, two miles south of Bradfield Corner. Built in 1908 by Joseph A. Britton of Burr Arch construction, this bridge is 54 feet long. A photographers dream!

The Bridges of Southeast Parke County
Bridgeton Bridge

This site describes a town, a mill, and a bridge. This is one of the spectacular stops in Parke County on County Road 780 South, west of Indiana 59. Several bridges and mills have been built on this location and generally fall victim to fire, flood, or changing times. The town is now an artist's colony of sorts, and is wide open for business during the festival.

The long (245 foot) double Burr Arch bridge was built over the cascades of Big Raccoon Creek in 1868. It is now bypassed for vehicles and preserved for walkers like you.

The roller mill built in 1868 is in operating condition and now sports a new coat of red paint.

Conley's Ford Bridge (top)

Crossing Big Raccoon Creek three miles south of Mansfield on Indiana 59, west on County Road 720 South, and north on 550 East, this is the only bridge by Jefferson Lawrence VanFosson. Constructed of double Burr Arch design, this 192-foot-long, single-span bridge was built in 1907.

Big Rocky Fork Bridge (bottom)

Built of Burr Arch construction in 1906 by Joseph J. Daniels, this 72-foot bridge was bypassed by the highway. Located on Big Rocky Creek south of Mansfield on Indiana 59, to County Road 726 South, then east two miles.

Jeffries Ford Bridge (top)

Located on the very edge of beautiful Pleasant Valley, this bridge can be found two miles southwest of Bridgeton on County road 890 South, then south on County road 150 East, where it crosses Big Raccoon Creek. Built in 1915 by Joseph A. Britton and Sons of twin span, Burr Arch design, this bridge is 204 feet in length. Sadly this bridge was destroyed by fire in 2002. Hopefully plans will soon be in place to restore the bridge to its original beauty.

Roseville-Coxville Bridge (bottom)

Built in 1910 by J. L. VanFosson in the Parke County bottoms, this double span, Burr Arch constructed bridge is 263 feet long. Located at the northern edge of Coxville on County Road 325 where it crosses Big Raccoon Creek.

The Bridges of Southwest Parke County
Harry Evans Bridge

Crossing Rock Run Creek three miles north of Rosedale on County Road 325 West, this bridge is in a very picturesque setting. Constructed by Joseph A. Britton in 1908 of Burr Arch design, this bridge is 65 feet long.

Adams Bridge

Mom and I were traveling, once again, the short distance to Indiana's Parke County Indiana's Covered Bridge Festival. Our main objective, to take photographs and experience the beauty of the covered bridges, not to shop today.

We traveled all the back roads. Avoiding traffic that way, and were successful. Of course, not without provocation.

I had never seen Adams Bridge in all the years I have visited Parke County. For good reason.

Mom and I turned off a road near Nyesville. The roads are small and one lane gravel. Sometimes there are road signs, and sometimes not. Around and around we went looking for this covered bridge. Once again, we returned to the same location. Once again, being lost.

Finally, we gave up. We became hungry. Stopping at a little café in Bellmore, we got smart, thinking the locals would be knowledgeable about the whereabouts of this bridge. The waitress was uncertain, but did not hesitate to ask other customers. Soon, the whole café was discussing the location of the bridge. No one was confident. We had several suggestions, but nothing concrete. We thought it a little peculiar no one knew of the bridge.

A man dressed up in DNR (Department of Natural Resources) clothing walked in for lunch. Boldly, I told Mom, "He, for sure, should know!" I proceeded to ask him. "Oh, that was the bridge that a flood took out quite a few years ago." "Is it where we drove over the creek on cement near Nyesville?" I asked. It was indeed.

So we gave up on that bridge, obviously, but continued on with our objectives. We headed toward Phillips Bridge.

Up a little hill and down, we could not believe our eyes? What a superb sight. The skies were perfectly blue; the bridge was centered flawlessly in the middle of the road, as if it was just beaming for people to photograph it. The autumn colors behind it were ideal. We felt elated. Ecstatic for what we had just viewed. We captured the moment a photographer always dreams of, the perfect setting, perfect lighting, and perfect peak seasonal moment. How lucky we felt.

"Wow! What a day," I said to Mom as we started our drive home. I then picked up our map; only to notice it was ten years old! "No wonder Adam's Bridge was gone! Think how many miles we went out of our way and drove to find it! Well, guess I will retire this map, huh Mom?" We laughed.

—Marsha Williamson Mohr

Thorpe Ford Bridge

Constructed in 1912 by Joseph A. Britton of double Burr Arch design, this bridge is 163 feet in length. Crossing Big Raccoon Creek, Thorpe Ford Bridge is located on the once busy Ben Hur Highway from Terre Haute to Crawfordsville, one mile northeast of Rosedale on County Road 40 East and 900 South.

Spencer and Perry Counties

These counties are veritable treasure troves of history. The Lincoln family, with their young son Abraham, crossed the Ohio River near Pigeon Creek in western Spencer County. They journeyed northward to Gentryville where they lived for the next fifteen years. Abraham grew to manhood there and, we would like to think, acquired his strong character from the rugged nature that surrounded him. The threat of white snakeroot milk poisoning, tradition has it, forced the family to relocate to New Salem, Illinois. The Lincoln Boyhood National Memorial at Lincoln City is a must on your travel itinerary. If you believe in famous people, you must see the town of Santa Claus and its Holiday World. Drive on up through the rolling countryside to see St. Meinard Abbey and its marvelous Old World architecture.

You can see the Huffman Mill Bridge in its rural setting on the way to Spencer County. Most of this county is part of Hoosier National Forest and offers great recreational opportunities.

Huffman Mill Bridge

Crossing the Anderson River on the northern edge of Huffman on the county line, this was the site of the Huffman sawmill in Lincoln's day. Built by William T. Washer in 1864 of Burr Arch construction, this well restored bridge in wooded surrounding is 140 feet in length.

Putnam County

This county is similar in many ways to Parke County, its neighbor to the west. It has a wealth of winding rural roads, pretty little towns, and a substantial livestock economy. Greencastle, the county seat, is a pretty town with DePauw University, one of America's leading liberal arts colleges. You should walk its campus and see newly renovated Meharry Hall.

The real jewel of Putnam County, however, is the Big Walnut River and its surrounding natural areas. The Big Walnut Nature Conservancy, just off U.S. 36, is a wooded paradise of virgin timber. About all the covered bridges in the county are on the Big Walnut.

Putnam County is different. It has beautiful rivers, awesome forest, and magnificent red bridges. I am going to present to you a gallery of Marsha Williamson Mohr's photographs of the bridges of Putnam County so that you can enjoy the beauty, uncluttered by facts. Then I will list the statistics for your reference. Ready, here we go!

The Bridges of Putnam County "Symphony in Red"

Cornstalk Bridge, Cornstalk Creek (top)

This 85-foot-long bridge was built in 1917 by J. A. Britton of Burr Arch Truss design. Cornstalk Bridge is located two miles north of Raccoon on County Road 1350 North.

Bakers Camp Bridge, Big Walnut Creek (bottom)

Built in 1901 by J. J. Daniels, this Burr Arch Truss design is 128 feet long. This bridge is located two miles southeast of Bainbridge on County Road 550 North in the Nature Preserve.

The Scene

A valley of an open pasture
Water flowing under
Trees hovering to its side
A structure hard to locate
Sometimes lengthy
Sometimes brief
A covered bridge is the construction I
am yearning to uncover

A lonely pastoral road
Winding to find its way
Forest joining the passage
A work of art I hope will stay

A warm feeling encompasses me from
times of yesteryear
I sit and stare at this scene and ask
What if you may, ask what and agree
Yes, yes, this is what life is all about

—Marsha Williamson Mohr

Dick Huffman Bridge, Big Walnut Creek

The oldest and longest bridge remaining in this county is located southwest of Manhattan, five miles on County Road 1050 South. Built in 1880, but builder unknown, the Dick Huffman Bridge is a double-span bridge of Howe Truss design, and is 265 feet long.

Dunbar Bridge, Big Walnut Creek
Located two miles north of Greencastle, just west of U.S. 231 on Dunbar Road, Dunbar Bridge is 174 feet long and is constructed of Burr Arch design. Built in 1880, but the builder is unknown.

Edna Collins Bridge, Little Walnut Creek
(opposite)
Built in 1922 by Charles Hendrix of Burr Arch Truss, this 80-foot-long bridge was the last public covered bridge built in Indiana. Located one mile northwest of Clinton Falls on County Road 450 North.

Rolling Stone Bridge, Big Walnut Creek (top)

Built of Burr Arch Truss in 1915 by J. A. Britton, this bridge is 103 feet long and is located two miles northeast of Bainbridge on County Road 800 North.

Houck Bridge, Big Walnut Creek (bottom)

Massillon Bridge Company built this double span, Howe Truss bridge that is 210 feet long. Located two miles south of Greencastle on Manhattan Road, west of County Road 550 South.

Oakalla Bridge, Big Walnut Creek (top)
Built in 1898 by J. J. Daniels, this Burr Arch Truss designed bridge is 152 feet long and is located two miles west of Limedale, north off County Road 300 South.

Pine Bluff Bridge, Big Walnut Creek (bottom)
Builder and date unknown for this Howe Truss, two spanned bridge that is 211 feet long. Located two and one-half miles north of Bainbridge near County Road 950 East.
NOTE: MANY PUTNAM COUNTY BRIDGES ARE HARD TO FIND! DON'T PANIC. USE YOUR COMPASS AND YOUR GAZETTEER ROAD MAP. ONE ODDITY, YOU WILL DISCOVER THAT ALL PUTNAM COUNTY BRIDGES HAVE VERTICAL SIDING AND DARK RED PAINT.

Ripley County

Ripley County is a transition county with the heavy clay flatlands to the north with grain and livestock farms, changing to the rugged hills of shale and limestone to the south. The southern area definitely longs to reach the Ohio River with its many small streams and narrow valleys. Laughery Creek of Indian massacre fame is its principal river. You certainly will want to visit the large and wooded Versailles State Park east of Versailles (pronounced Versayles in Hoosier) on U.S. 50. Don't miss the spectacular art-deco Methodist Church in Versailles, built by the founder of the Walgreen Drug Store chain. He was born and raised there. If you are a muzzleloader fan, check on the many events that take place at their shooting grounds at Friendship.

Holton or Otter Creek Bridge

Located west of Holton on Versailles Road, then go north on Canal Bridge Road where it crosses Otter Creek. Built by Thomas A. Hardman in 1884, this 102-foot-long bridge is constructed of Howe Truss design, and has been beautifully restored and painted bright red!

Busching Bridge

Located at the south entrance to Versailles State Park, this bridge is 176 feet long and crosses Laughery Creek. Busching Bridge was built in 1885 by Thomas A. Hardman and was constructed of Howe Truss design.

Rush County

This county is one of the richest agricultural counties in America. Proud old farms, with huge livestock barns and Victorian houses, have been in the same families for generations. Historically they are producers of fine herds of hogs, beef cattle, and sheep, and they still do, I might add.

Likewise, for Rush County, quality, beauty, and strength were just as important for its covered bridges. From 1870 to 1918, three generations of the A. M. Kennedy family built bridges that most anyone could tell at a glance.

These were always white, had horizontal lap siding, and the portals were always decorated with a delicately carved archway, elaborate covered roof braces, and complex filigree trim. Early large bridges in Connersville, Rushville, and Shelbyville were signature pieces to the professional pride of the Kennedy clan. They were beautiful objects of art with sidewalks, gracefully colonnaded entrances and balustrades and complete sidewalk railings. They were a joy to behold, but sadly the elaborate "village" bridges in those cities are all gone.

There was an Archibald Kennedy, the scion, Emmett and Charles, his sons, and Charles and Karl, grandsons to follow.

Nearly a dozen Kennedy bridges have survived to this day, mostly in eastern Indiana.

Smith Bridge

A. M. Kennedy and Sons built this 136-foot-long bridge of Burr Arch Truss design, in 1877. Crossing Flatrock River, the Smith Bridge is located northeast of Rushville on County Road 100 East, then turning east on County Road 150 North.

Offutt Ford Bridge

Offutts Ford Bridge is located on County Road 450 West, east of Arlington, north to County Road 300 North, turn west then north on Offutts Ford Road. Built by the Kennedy Brothers over the little Blue River in 1884, this bridge is of Burr Arch Truss and is 98 feet long.

Moscow Bridge

Moscow Bridge is located in Moscow! Built by Emmett L. Kennedy in 1886, this bridge crosses Flatrock River, and is 334 feet long.

Forsythe or Forsythe Mill Bridge (top)

Built in 1888 across the Flatrock River by Emmett Kennedy, this Burr Arch Truss designed bridge is 197 feet long. Forsythe Bridge is located northeast of Moscow on County Road 840 South, north on County Road 500 West for two miles.

Norris/Norris Ford Bridge (bottom)

Norris Ford Bridge is located northeast of Rushville on County Road 175 North, east on County Road 300 North. Built by E. M. Kennedy and Sons in 1916, this bridge crosses Flatrock River.

Homer Bridge/Homer Barn Bridge

Homer Barn Bridge is located on private property on the southeast edge of Homer, where it was converted to a barn. A flood washed out the original bridge in 1892, after being built in 1881 by an unknown builder. NOTE: THE LAST KENNEDY BRIDGE WAS BUILT IN 1918 NEAR FOUNTAIN CITY IN WAYNE COUNTY, INDIANA. IT NO LONGER EXISTS.

Scott County

Scott County changes as you drive south on Interstate 65 toward Louisville, from a wet lowland bottom of the Muscatatuck River to a valley running along the dramatic Floyd Knobs area. Then, you enter the rush and the crowds of the Falls City area. While you're down that way, drive Indiana 160 from Salem to Charlestown. It takes time, but the scenery is well worth the effort.

Rural Scott County has one real claim to fame. The little town of Leota has the newest covered bridge in Indiana, maybe in the nation. If you want to get them all, you will need this one.

Leota Bridge

Located in Leota on County Road 400 West, southwest of Scottsburg, turn southeast on Bloomington Trail Road. Built in 1995 by L. L. Brown Construction Company, this bridge crosses Cooney Creek and has two lanes 37 feet long.

Vermillion County

This county is an unusual place! For one thing it is one township wide and eight townships longs. At the north end you can eat at the Beef House, one of Indiana's great restaurants, or you can eat in your overalls at a good place in Eugene. You can see glimpses of black Illinois prairies at Dana and Gessie. The Vermillion River cuts across its middle, creating hills and hollows: good places for covered bridges. In the south end, you will find where strip mines used to be. Vermillion County is almost Illinois prairie on the west; almost coal country on the south, and kind of like Parke County on the east. It's an interesting place. Drive Indiana 63 from one end to the other!

Vermillion County honors the birthplace of Ernie Pyle of World War II fame at Dana, has large wintering colonies of eagles at Cayuga, and a huge repository for nerve gas. Now Newport even has a crossroads called Flat Iron. You'll see several covered bridges and a place where a bridge used to be.

Eugene Bridge

Eugene Bridge is located north of Cayuga on County Road 00 East where it crosses the Vermillion River. Built of Burr Arch Truss design in 1885 by J. J. Daniels, this bridge is 192 feet in length. There's a good place to eat close to the bridge!

Newport Bridge

J. J. Daniels built the 180-foot-long bridge of Burr Arch construction, in 1885. Crossing the Little Vermillion River, Newport Bridge is located one mile west of Newport, just west of Indiana 63.

Hillsdale-Possum Bridge (above)

Moved from Hillsdale to rest park on U.S. 36, two miles east of Dana, this Burr Arch Truss designed bridge is 104 feet in length. This is also a J. J. Daniels bridge built in 1876.

South Hill Bridge (opposite)

For the surprise of your life, take County Road 1680 South-southwest of Clinton. It turns into a beautiful brick road. Drive for about three miles and you will come to Brouilette Creek, where the bridge used to be. The bridge is now stored in the park at St. Bernice. The plans are for it to be reconstructed in 2002.

Vigo County

Terre Haute and its environs create a distinctly urban setting in Western Indiana's Vigo County. In the face of rapid industrialization, the folks over there have never lost sight of the past. In Fowler Park, they have recreated a pioneer village, complete with a brand new gristmill, many pioneer log homes and businesses, and have moved in a fine covered bridge, Irishman Bridge from Riley. You must see it and the rest of the park as well.

Irishman Bridge

Moved from Honey Creek west of Riley to Fowler Park, it is now located ten miles south of Terre Haute on U.S. 41 and then east. Watch for the sign. Built by C. W. Bishop in 1845 of Modified Queen Post Truss, this bridge is 75 feet in length. Another good bridge saved!

Wabash County

Wabash County is rather representative of the fertile flat Tipton Till plain in central Indiana. If you like to drive rural farm roads, take Indiana 26 from Lafayette to Fairmount and beyond. It doesn't take must imagination to understand why this is called "The Cornbelt." The pristine Eel River angles across the middle of Wabash County, North Manchester, with its shady broad streets, magnificent old homes, prestigious Manchester College and impressive North Manchester Bridge anchor the river on the north. Downstream (southwest) the Eel River shows you its vital connection to the history of the area. In times past, this verdant valley was a beehive of activity; farmers were building huge pin-frame barns, prime cattle grazing the creek banks, with deer, beaver, and blue herons sharing the joy of the river. Huge gristmills rumbled with activity with loaded farm wagons driving through graceful covered bridges. Drive Indiana 16 across Wabash County. You'll see Indiana at its best. Don't miss the beautiful bridges at North Manchester and Roann. Watch for the remains of a great old mill around Stockdale. Indiana would appear to be international with Peru, Chili, and Mexico a few of the towns in this area.

North Manchester Bridge

This village bridge on the Eel River is located in the southeast part of North Manchester at South Mill and Sycamore Streets. Built by Smith Bridge Company in 1872 of Smith No. 4 Truss, this bridge is 150 feet in length. It formerly had a pedestrian way!

Roann Bridge

Roann Bridge crosses the Eel River, just north of Roann on County Road 700 West. Built by Smith Bridge Company in 1877 of Howe Truss construction, this bridge has two spans of 288 feet. Suffering a disastrous fire in 1990, the bridge was completely rebuilt by Amos Schwartz, renowned barn and bridge restorer. It now has a sprinkler system.

Index

A
Adams County, 20–21
Adams Mill Bridge, 34, 35
Anderson River, 128
Auburn Cord-Duesenberg Auto Museum, 42

B
Bakers Camp Bridge, 130, 160
Baron & Hole, 68
Bartholomew County, 22
Bean Blossom Bridge, 27
Bean Blossom Creek, 27
Beeson Bridge, 106
Bells Ford Bridge, 64
Big Bayou Creek, 55
Big Raccoon Creek, 109, 120, 123, 124, 125, 127
Big Rocky Creek, 124
Big Rocky Fork Bridge, 124
Big Shawnee Creek, 46
Big Walnut Nature Conservancy, 130
Big Walnut River, 130
Billie Creek Bridge, 105
Billie Creek Village, 86, 105, 106
Billy Creek Village Historical Museum, 8
Bishop, C. W., 152
Blue River, 142
Bluffs of Sugar Creek, 77–78
Bowsher Ford Bridge, 95
Bridges of the Past, Historic Landmarks of Parke County, 13
Bridgeton Bridge, 122, 123
Britton, Joseph A., builder, 16, 86, 92, 94, 95, 98, 100, 101, 106, 114, 116, 121, 125, 126, 127, 130, 134
Brouilette Creek, 150
Brown Construction Company, L. L., 146
Brown County State Park, 24, 26
Brown County, 24–27
Burr Arch Truss, 18
Busching Bridge, 138–139

C
Cades Mill Bridge, 47
Caitlin Bridge, 120
Carroll County, 28–37
Cataract Falls Bridge, 84–85
Cataract Falls States Recreation Area, 84
Cataract Falls, 82–83
Cedar Chapel Bridge, 61
Ceylon Bridge, 20, 21
Children's Museum, 74
Clinton Falls, 132
Coal Creek, 47
Conley's Ford Bridge, 124
Conner Prairie Settlement, 60, 61
Cornstalk Bridge, endsheet, 130
Covered Bridge Festival, 6, 86
Cox Ford Bridge, 94
Crooks Bridge, 104
Crosley Fish and Wildlife area, 68
Cumberland Bridge, 57

D
Daniels, Joseph J., builder, 16, 65, 66, 73, 80, 86, 96, 99, 105, 109, 114, 116, 120, 124, 130, 135, 148, 149, 150
Darlington Bridge, 79
Dean, James, 56
Dearborn County, 38
Decatur County, 40, 41
Deer's Mill Bridge, 80–81
DeKalb County, 42
Dick Huffman Bridge, 131
Duck Creek, 48, 48
Dunbar Bridge, 132
Durfee, Josiah, 61, 75

E
Edna Collins Bridge, cover, 15, 133
Eel River, 154, 155
Eiteljorg, 74
Erie Canal, 97
Essential Parts, 18, 19
Eugene Bridge, 148

F
Fairgrounds Bridge, 70, 71
Fayette County, 44
Fishback Creek, 74
Flatrock River, 140, 143, 144
Forsythe or Forsythe Mill Bridge, 144
Fountain County, 46
Fowler Park, 152

Frankfort Construction Company, *106*
Franklin County, 16, 48

G
Gibson County, 54–55
Graham Creek, 68
Grant County, 56–57
Greene County, 58–59
Guilford Bridge, 7, 38, *39*

H
Hamilton County, 60–61
Hardman, Thomas A., 136, 138
Harry Evans Bridge, *126*
Hendricks, William, builder, *93*, *97*
Hendrix, Charles, *132*
Henry County, 15
Highland Park, 62, *62*
Hillsdale–Possum Bridge, *150*
Holton or Otter Creek Bridge, 136, *137*
Homer Bridge/Homer Barn Bridge, *145*
Honey Creek, *152*
Houck Bridge, *134*
Howard County, 62–63
Howe Truss, 18
Huffman Mill Bridge, *128 129*

I
Indiana State Fair, 74
Indianapolis Museum of Art, The, 74
Irishman Bridge, *152*, *153*

J
Jackson Bridge, *96*
Jackson County, 64–67
James Bridge, *69*
Jeffries Ford Bridge, *125*
Jennings County, 68–69
Johnson's Creek, *52*

K
Kankakee River, 70
Kennedy and Sons, A. M., builder, 16, 38, *41*, *44*, *58*, *70*, *140*, *142*, *144*
Kennedy, Emmett L., *143*, *144*
Kress, Joseph, *79*

L
Lake County, 70–71
Lancaster Bridge, *36*, *37*
Lawrence County, 72–73
Leather Creek, *106*
Leatherwood Bridge, 8
Leatherwood Creek, *116*
Leatherwood Station Bridge, *106*
Leota Bridge, *146*, *147*
Lieber Park, Richard, *84*
Lincoln Boyhood National Memorial, 128
Little Raccoon Creek, *99*, *100*, *101*, *104*, *113*, *114*
Little Vermilion River, *149*
Longwood Bridge, *45*

M
Mansfield Bridge and Mill, *107–109*
Maple Syrup Festival, 86
Marion County, 74–75
Marshall Bridge, *98*
Massillon Bridge Company, *134*
McAllister Bridge, *101*
McDaniel, Clark, *120*
Mecca Bridge, *120*
Medora Bridge, *66*, *67*
Melcher Bridge, *116*
Mill Creek, *82*, *95*, *97*
Mill Creek-Tow Path Bridge, *97*
Mill Race Park, 22
Mississinawa River, 56
Montgomery County, 76–81
Moscow Bridge, *143*
Muscatatuck Creek, 68
Muscatatuck River, 146

N
Narrows Bridge, The, *92*, back cover
National Road Bridge, 74
National Road, 15
Neet Bridge, *99*
Nevins Bridge, *100*
New Brownsville Bridge, 22, *23*
Newport Bridge, *149*
Norris/Norris Ford Bridge, *144*
North Manchester Bridge, *154*

O

Oakalla Bridge, *135*
Offutt Ford Bridge, *142*
Old Red Bridge, *55*
Otter Creek Golf Course, 22
Otter Creek, 136
Owen County, 82–85

P

Parke County, 6, 16, 86–127
Patoka River National Wildlife Reserve, *54*
Patoka River, *54*
Phillips or Arabia Bridge, 119
Pine Bluff Bridge, *135*
Portland Arch Nature Preserve, 46
Portland Mills Bridge, *111*
Potter's Bridge, *61*
Putnam County, 15, 16, 130–135

R

Ramp Creek Bridge, *26*
Richland-Plummer Creek Bridge, *58, 59*
Ripley County, 136–139
Roann Bridge, *155*
Roaring Creek, *106*
Rob Roy Bridge, *46*
Roberts Park, 44
Rock Run Creek, *121, 126*
Rolling Stone Bridge, *134*
Roseville-Coxville Bridge, *125*
Rush County, 16, 140–145
Rush Creek Bridge, *97*
Rush Creek, *98*

S

Salt Creek, 26, *53*
Sanatorium Bridge, 7, *114*
Sand Creek, 40, *41, 68*
Scipio Bridge, *68*
Scott County, 146, 147
Seal Barn Bridge, 50, 51
Seasons at McAllister Bridge, *102–103*
Seasons of Portland Mills Bridge, *112–113*
Seasons on Sugar Creek, *90–91*
Seymour Bridge Company, *64*
Shades State Park, 76, *80*
Shelby County, 16
Shieldstone Bridge, *65*

Sim Smith Bridge, *116, 117*
Smith Bridge Company, 57, *154, 155*
Smith Bridge, *140–141*
Smith Truss, 18
Snow Hill Bridge, *52*, 150, *151*
Spencer and Perry Counties, 128
Spencerville Bridge, 42, *43*
Stockheughter Bridge, *53*
Sugar Creek, 76, *92, 94, 96, 114*
Sugar Mill Creek, *47*

T

Thorpe Ford Bridge, *127*
Traders Point Bridge, *75*
Turkey Run State Park, *92, 93, 94*

V

VanFosson, Jefferson Lawrence, builder, *124, 125*
Vermillion County, 16, 148–151
Vermont Bridge, *62, 63*
Versailles State Park, 136, 138
Vigo County, 152, 153

W

Wabash County, 154
Wabash River, 20, 46, 54, *114*
Wallace Bridge, *46*, 47
Washer, William T., builder, *54*, 128
Weaver Popcorn Company, 56
West Union Bridge, 114, *115*
Westport Bridge, 40, *41*
Wheeling Bridge, *54*
Wheelock Bridge Company, *35, 36*
White River State Park and Zoo, 74
White River, 54, 60, 64, 82
Whitewater Canal Aqueduct, *48, 49*
Whitewater Canal, 48, *48*
Whitewater River, 48
Wildcat Creek, 28, *36*
Wilkins Mill Bridge, *93*
Williams Bridge, 73
Williams Creek, *106*
Woentz and Son, George, *42*
Wolf, Aaron, builder, *26*
Wolfe, Henry, *104, 112*

Z

Zacke Cox Bridge, *121*

About the Authors

Marsha Williamson Mohr

Marsha Williamson Mohr has actively been taking photographs for some fifteen years. She has had many of her photographs in publications such as *Country*, *Farm and Ranch Living*, *Indiana*, and *Virginia Tour Guides*, on postcards, calendars, in books and catalogues. Her "Claim to Fame" is photographing rural scenes and structures, even though she will have an occasional mountain or autumn scene published. Marsha's photographs are recognized by her style. Her work composing these unique rural scenes are what she aspires for; viewing, striving, arranging over and over until it's perfect, with her own individual inventive technique.

Marrying her high school sweetheart Larry, they enjoy their two children, Heather and Cameron. Being outside playing tennis, bicycling, skiing, or jogging fits their active lifestyle.

Marsha claims to have the best two jobs anyone could ask for. She is also a registered nurse working at a local hospital in acute care settings. The hands on caring, and making a difference in one roll; being alone, photographing the country, seeing the sights and sounds of nature, and creating a massive library of images, in the other.

Photo by Richard G. Biever

Maurice L. Williamson

Maurice L. (Mauri) Williamson just might be one of the last of the "good old boys." Raised on a general livestock farm in Wayne County, Indiana, he suffered through the hard times of the Depression, milked a whole lot of cows, and got pretty good at shooting baskets up against the barn. He learned the joy of success and the agony of defeat in 4-H, and found the farm a wonderful place to embrace the wonders of nature, and the values gained from a communal experience with the traditions of the past.

After serving in the Navy in World War II, Mauri entered the School of Agriculture at Purdue University, and excelled in the life sciences, communication, and leadership.

After graduation, he labored on the home farm for a few years, and then returned to Purdue as executive secretary of the Agricultural Alumni Association serving in the post for almost forty years.

As leader of that large and effective agricultural society, he assumed a prominent role in the professional leadership in agriculture programs throughout the Midwest. He was a popular after dinner speaker, and was a prolific writer of organizational treatises and articles.

In 1961, he organized the Pioneer Farm and Home Show at the Indiana State Fair, and remains the manager of that immensely successful living history museum to this day. It attracts over 200,000 visitors during the twelve-day run of the Fair.

In 1994, he founded the Center for Agricultural Science and Heritage, a dream that has become a nationally recognized forum for education, advocacy, and preservation for his beloved agricultural profession.

He is active in many preservation societies, and fervently stands on the podium of effective action on farming's behalf.

After retirement, he continues to speak, write, and act for good causes of all kinds. He still walks the fields of his beloved farm, operated under the name "David Williamson and Dad."